Love to Ann

from Eileen Hill.

CURTAIN UP, CURTAIN DOWN

Curtain Up, Curtain Down

Eileen Hartly Hodder

Sansom &
Company

First published in 1999 by Sansom & Company Ltd.,
81g Pembroke Road, Bristol BS8 3EA

© Eileen Hartly Hodder

ISBN 1 900178 17 6

British Cataloguing-in-Publication Data.
A catalogue record for this book is available from the British Library.

Typeset by Mayhew Typesetting, Rhayader, Powys and printed
by WBC, Bridgend, Mid Glamorgan.

Contents

Acknowledgements

My thanks go to several people: Pamela and James Allcock, Greta Bickerton, Eunice Bliss, Michael Dickman, Michael Gibbs, Margaret and Peter Hibbs, Simon Mallitte and to Derek Clark and his film crew.

I also want to thank Sue Gallaugher for her encouragement and Liz Marleyn and Anne Mallitte respectively for editing and presenting my manuscript in a form suitable for me to offer to my publisher, John Sansom.

Foreword

I count it a great privilege to be asked to write a foreword to this book.

One is very fortunate in life to encounter a great teacher in one's early formative years. I was so blessed in 1941 when I went to my first lesson in 'elocution', as it was rather primly termed in those days, with Eileen Hartly Hodder at Weirfield School in Taunton; that word 'elocution' does not begin to describe the scope and impact of those lessons. Diction and clarity of speech were certainly dealt with, but so were breathing, phrasing, tone, verse structure and all the elements and disciplines of the art of verse speaking.

I continued my tuition with Eileen at her studio in Bristol, travelling daily from Glastonbury to do so, and through her firm guidance (and firm she certainly could be!) came to view the speaking of poetry as a natural and liberating means of expression, rather than a task to be feared.

She coached me in some pieces for my RADA audition, one of which was a poem – Shelley's 'The Cloud'. I have read this poem many, many times over the years in recital programmes, and have never failed to be aware of Eileen at my shoulder, shaping my interpretation, for this is what fine teachers do, they stay with you all your life, guiding and supporting long after their physical presence has been left behind.

Eventually, I left that indomitable little lady behind in Bristol and embarked on my RADA studies, where I found several tutors separately teaching me things I had learned in one package with her! Perhaps an unfair advantage, but how fortunate to have had such a wonderful grounding.

And here is your book, dear Eileen, with memories and anecdotes from your long and so productive life, a life that has had such an influence on mine for over half a century. I thank you Eileen, my friend for all these years, on behalf of all those to whom you have been such a help and inspiration.

God bless you.

Barbara Jefford

Dedicated to Carolyn Harman, without whose loving and constant care this book would never have been written and published.

Prologue
A Country House in Gloucestershire, 1905

I remember it all so clearly, the footsteps overhead and the susurration of voices, no-one to give me breakfast, "Mummy," I called, "Nanny." There was no answer. In fury I hurled my egg across the table where it made a lovely yellow splodge, then I was aghast, I thought that Nanny would be cross, I'd better hide. So I tottered through the open front door and squeezed uncomfortably into the shelter of a huge laurel bush. Soon voices began to call but I stayed silent and I suppose I must have fallen asleep until later, hungry, I calmly emerged. I was two and a half, the date was August 25th 1905, my brother John had been born that morning. I am Eileen, the only daughter of Mr. and Mrs. C. Hartly Hodder of Middleton House, Gloucestershire – the C stands for Clement, a family named hated by my father and never used.

Hodder is an old Saxon word meaning gently flowing river and Hodder families can be found beside waters in various parts of England. We always imagined that our ancestors came from Somerset as there is a Hodderscombe near Taunton, but there were at least six generations in Gloucestershire so it is quite a saddening thought to know that I am the last of the clan.

My father, nicknamed Michael, was born in Middleton House, Gloucestershire in 1874, the third generation of Hodders to live in the house. I don't really know where he went to school, somewhere in Bristol I fancy. I only know that he was a wonderful horseman and sportsman and a man of incredible courage.

He was very proud of being the first man in Gloucestershire to have a car, a Scat, and a driving licence; unfortunately the licence, as indeed all our family papers, went up in smoke during World War II in a direct hit on the office in Queen Square, Bristol. His father was a martinet, very strict, and father was brought up with a frequent horsewhipping for everything that he did that was wrong. His young sister, Lallie, prevailed upon her father to allow her to train as an opera singer in London, she had a most beautiful voice. So she went to the Royal College of Music, where strangely enough my mother had also prevailed upon her family to allow her to go to study piano.

Lallie and my mother formed a great friendship which lasted all their lives and one day father, going to see Lallie, arrived just as my mother, Edith, joined her and he immediately said to himself, "I'm going to marry that girl". He wasn't very tall but very good looking and with tremendous charm, and my mother – she was only seventeen at the time, being totally ignorant of men and the ways of the world – fell in love with him. I'm pretty sure she didn't fall in love with the country, though I do know that she insisted on having a bathroom installed in Middleton House. One of my great aunts, Maud, had married Mortimer Singer, a member of the immensely wealthy American family who invented the sewing machine. Mortimer was well in advance of his time and insisted when my parents married that my mother had a separate income which she controlled.

My father was exceedingly generous, as his father had been before him, but it was enormously useful to have a wealthy wife. So my mother went to this charming little house in Gloucestershire with a wonderful view right across the timber pond (I must explain that the timber pond – now vanished – was a huge pit filled with water in which planks of wood were left to weather until they were ready for use), the canal, the River Severn to Wales. When I went there some three years ago and rediscovered the house, to my delight that view remains uninterrupted.

My father was a partner in the family shipping firm and ran the offices at Sharpness, Gloucester and later, Bristol and Avonmouth. He was quite a lot older than my mother, and when in later days he took us to hotels, the receptionist always said, "I presume the single room is for you, sir, and your daughters will be in the double room," a question which always annoyed him intensely. They entertained enormously, the house was always full of visitors and usually they were made to work, because I remember that we had a croquet lawn which was immediately outside the drawing room and they decided that they would make a tennis court out of part of the orchard; my father and all his friends used to spend weekends levelling this patch of ground. There was a lot of land attached to the house; in those days we had stables and a yard where animals were kept. There was a farm attached to the house so we always had our own butter, cream and eggs.

I remember Nanny, but I never knew a cook because we were never allowed out into the kitchen. We had a manservant, who was valet to my father, and two or three gardeners and a couple of grooms.

My mother, married at 20, was a wonderful woman and had an enormous influence on me all my life. We were devoted to each other. She was very quiet, never raising her voice, but she exuded disapproval and you

10

knew when she was angry and you wouldn't go any further. She was a very wealthy woman and always insisted on managing her own financial affairs; she brought me up to say that to be wealthy was a great privilege and you should always spend a third of your income helping other people. When she died and I had to go through all her papers, I was astounded at the immense charity work she had supported. She was a strange mixture of shrewdness and simplicity. I remember when my father died, she wanted to go to London the next week, and she said to me, "How shall I get there?" It was during the war, so she couldn't get there by car, so I said, "By train, of course!" but she said, "How do I go by train?" I said, "You must get a ticket." "Ticket," she said, "where, how?" So I had to ring up the office and ask them to get a first class ticket for her because she had no idea at all how to get one.

Yet she was extraordinarily able, because she started the Ladies Lifeboat Guild in Bristol: single-handed she organised the flag day – nowadays we have a whole committee to do it – so you can see that she had a very good business mind, if only she had been allowed to use it. She was always very elegant, her clothes were made for her by Worth in Paris. Her parents lived in London: my grandfather, Joseph, a dear, good-tempered chap from Bridlington, was a barrister and my grandmama Baron had wit and intelligence, and wonderful hair – as a matter of fact all the females on either side had good hair ranging from very blonde to red-gold and apparently they could all sit on it! This must have been a Victorian virtue – mine never grew beyond my shoulder blades, to my great grief. Alas, in company with her sisters, my grandmother became an alcoholic and when she died my mother found every drawer and cupboard full of port bottles, empty of course. My grandmama's brothers were all inventors and engineers. One, Eustace, invented many kinds of machines. Another, John, invented the Artillery wheel, for which he was made a Freeman of the City of London. All these uncles were painted by various artists, good and indifferent, and hung later in my dining room. They now line the hall and staircase of my niece Jann.

My Granny Hodder was an Evans, with a brother and three sisters whom I never knew. Grandpa Hodder looked and seemed to us a benevolent old man, but as I mentioned earlier he was extremely strict with my father. He and his ancestors before him had always been connected with the sea and particularly with the River Severn, with offices in Gloucester and Sharpness for generations. Indeed he owned the first steam tug to ply between the two ports. By the time I was born he had opened an office in Bristol, which my father took over and later extended to Avonmouth.

11

Grandpa had two gentle and older sisters who worked at Mullers Orphanage; whenever they visited us we had to hide all signs of drink or cards!

When I was born, my parents decided to choose the most delightful and wealthiest of their friends and relations to be my godparents, so my aunt Maud Singer became my godmother and my godfather was one Joe Fawcett, a charming and lovely man, six foot and Saville Row-suited, who always wore a monocle. (My father later affected this but he never carried it off!) Later Uncle Joe, to my father's consternation, took to inviting me out to lunch, so I became accustomed at an early age to the best tables at the Ritz and the Savoy.

My aunt Maud with her husband, Mortimer Singer, just knighted as a pioneer of plane and motor car development, soon settled in England and eventually the two daughters married, one the Prince de Polignac, and the other, the Duc de Cazes. So we were occasionally invited to their various mansions in Paris and Biarritz. Daisy, the daughter of the de Cazes, married Sir Reginald Fellowes, whose grandson was until recently one of the Queen's chief advisors. Mortimer had a brother with an estate bordering on Goodwood race course so we saw a good deal of racing. Another bought a house in Paignton. Yet another took Isadora Duncan as his mistress in Paris but nobody ever spoke of him! Then Mortimer bought, in turn, two beautiful yachts, first the *Mary Maund* and then the *White Heather*, so we had plenty of sailing in most luxurious conditions. Alas, Aunt Mary died in 1930 without leaving a will, and dear Uncle Joe went bankrupt in the Depression and committed suicide by throwing himself under a train.

Middleton House was a very pretty house. The dining room to the left as we entered was Regency pink: we called it the Red room because it was so unusual to have anything but dark green paint in those days. (When I renewed my friendship with the house some ninety years later, I found that the present delightful owners, the Hales, are using the same colour.) The drawing room ran the length of the right side of the building and had windows and a door leading out onto a croquet lawn, where at one end there was a huge tree. I believe it was a kind of cherry and I still remember the pink blossoms blowing down on us as we sat on the swing, guarded as always by our wonderful bulldog called Fitz (after the occupant of Berkeley Castle). John and I also had a goat and a little goat-chaise in which we wandered through the lanes. As children John and I would run down to the River Severn and bring back pails full of wriggling white 'worms'. Elvers are now extremely expensive and are bought by the Japanese and other distant purchasers at vast prices.

There was no central heating, so it was frightfully cold. Both John and I had terrible chilblains on hands and feet. I dreaded the treatment for this because Nanny would plunge our feet into a bowl of very hot water with mustard melted in it. We longed to become really ill so that we could have wood fires in our bedrooms. I think that mother would have given us these all winter through but my father was made of sterner stuff and thought we ought to be toughened by having cold baths. Horrors!

Nanny was loved by everyone; she moved with us to Bristol where she became my mother's personal maid, which meant of course that she was my maid as well. So I never tidied my room or brushed my hair – very bad training. The cook was a fat country-woman, very pleasant, who cooked all the strange country dishes enjoyed by my father – tripe, chitterlings, black pudding, pigs' trotters. I can remember only one of the grooms, the one who looked after my pony Charlie. He slept in the house, in the loft, which was divided into three: a large space for the apples, a small room for the groom and a larger one with two beds where Daddy's various male friends spent weekends. I was fascinated by the apple smell which influenced my subsequent enjoyment of Drinkwater's 'Moonlit Apples'. There were also attractive young men and sometimes I crept upstairs, although I was specifically warned not to do so, and once woke an occupant by crawling into his bed. When he realised what was happening, he lay rigid, with closed eyes, until I got tired of the adventure and never disturbed him again.

To go back to 1905, I hated my brother and treated him abominably, he was a delicate baby and I was a boringly bouncing healthy child. Once I nearly killed him by hurling a china doll at him from the landing; fortunately, as always, my aim was very poor and so I missed him and it smashed to smithereens on the hall floor. This dreadful jealousy continued for several years until one day picnicking on Nibley Hill with Tyndall's Monument towering above us, I inadvertently allowed him to get above me during a struggle with the result that he threw me to the ground; thereafter I treated him with considerably more respect.

The next exciting thing I remember was the wedding of my father's sister, Alice Mabel, always called Lallie, to Cuthbert Hicks. He worked with his father, the editor of the *Western Daily Press*. My grandparents disapproved of him but we children all adored him because he played cricket with us and made jokes which we understood. I always remember the day when one of my gentle Hodder aunts said reprovingly to Lallie, 'change the name and not the letter' and Cuthbert immediately quipped, "it can't be for worse so it must be for better".

By this time I was five and I was a train bearer. Cuthbert's sister, Winifred (a militant Suffragette), was chief bridesmaid and one of his nephews, Coldstream Tuckett, was page by my side. Apparently I embarrassed the latter greatly throughout the service by begging him to marry me! The wedding took place at Berkeley Church, the service was conducted by one of Grannie's nephews, St. John Evans, and the festivities were held at Middleton House on a beautiful spring day. The new Mr and Mrs Hicks drove off in a carriage and the best man followed in our pony and trap – unfortunately he fell out, completely drunk.

My first Meet was in the October of that year. I was kitted out in great style: a velvet jockey cap, my father insisting that my curls were plaited, so they must have stuck out like little rats' tails; brown leather riding boots which were displayed in a Bond Street window as the smallest pair ever made. I rode my roan pony, while my father, in his mustard Berkeley colours, was mounted on his black stallion.

The Meet was on the top of Nibley Hill and we had to draw in to the sides of the narrow lane as the Master, Lord Fitz-Harding, arrived. My pony became very excited, this was his first Meet too. My groom had me on a leading rein but because he met many of his cronies he became somewhat careless and as soon as the huntsman blew his horn, Charlie galloped down the steep hill to be faced with a five-bar gate at the bottom. He didn't like the look of that so he stopped abruptly and I pitched over his head, over the gate and into the mud!

My father and I adored horses, and my mother, looking very elegant, rode side-saddle on her chestnut, Jacko. John disliked horses – to my father's disappointment because he was a wonderful horseman who could drive a four-in-hand and a tandem with equal ease. One of the family anecdotes was how a friend bet him a hundred pounds, then a vast sum, that he couldn't beat the train to London. So one fine day he left Berkeley Road Station as the guard blew his whistle and the train steamed out for Paddington. My father, the story went, arrived at Marble Arch just half a minute before the train steamed in to Paddington.

Another exciting memory of that period was my first visit to Drury Lane to see *Cinderella*, with real white ponies and Dorothy Ward as Principal Boy. She had wonderful legs which I still remember. I was enraptured by the entire experience so at the end of the performance one of my cousins said she could take me backstage. Suddenly everything changed and became hateful; we hurried along black, cold passages, opened Cinderella's door to find – nothing. No wonderful clothes, no Prince, no make-up, only a very

14

ordinary bedraggled girl in a dressing gown. No wonder I howled, but somehow the magic seed was sown and from that day the theatre became my main interest and delight.

Once John and I went to London to stay with Grandmama on our own. I suppose Father must have been ill so Nanny was needed at home to nurse him. The very first morning we were sent unaccompanied into the bathroom; of course, at once we locked the door and proceeded to have a water battle, so that the place became a lake, while we ignored the rattles and shouts of our unfortunate grandparents. When the water grew colder and we grew hungry, we were forced to open the door and face our infurated relations. I can't remember how we were punished, probably taken out breakfastless for a walk.

The next afternoon some of our young cousins were brought in to tea. They were a little younger than we were and were boringly well brought up, never speaking unless they were spoken to. Well, we sat down to tea and by this time I had developed a cold and sniffed incessantly. I was born with very narrow nasal passages so could never blow my nose properly. Grandpapa kept lending me a handkerchief to no effect, so he unwisely said, "John doesn't sniff, John will show you how to do it." Whereupon John, the better to show off, stood up on his chair and blew with such force that he fell and hit his nose on the table, causing it to bleed profusely – to my great delight. By this time Nanny had arrived and broke up the party by insisting that we were both sent to bed.

My cousin Maud was married to Sir George Bagerow, then the foremost surgeon in London for ear, nose and throat disorders. He kindly offered to operate on me, so next morning I was taken to his consulting rooms where he anaesthetised my nose and throat and thrust a red hot wire up both passages. It didn't hurt but as the drug wore off the mucous of years cascaded down, so I had to stay in bed for the rest of the week. This certainly relieved the pressure so that I no longer sniffed, but I've never been able to blow my nose properly and I always insist on performing this task in private.

On a typical summer's day at home we would get up early to trot behind my father in the dog cart, then back to a large breakfast and half an hour's practice, John on the nursery piano, me on the drawing room grand. Then biscuits and milk followed by an hour's work with a governess. We spoke French always to our French governess and German to our solitary Hun. Then out to play in the garden, mostly on the swing, which of course we quarrelled over. We stayed out there until lunch-time. In the afternoon we went round the lanes sometimes venturing as far as Frampton-on-Severn with its wonderful village green where we occasionally called on a very old couple called the de Lacey-Evans, distant relations of my grandmother. Back to tea in the drawing room where my mother usually had guests.

Then to bath-time and listening enthralled while Mother read the Beatrix Potter books. By the age of five I knew most of them by heart and corrected her if she deviated by a syllable. Then a romp with Father and so to bed to argue and quarrel with John over everything. If he said it was so, I said it was not. These constant arguments so irritated our parents that from a very early age we were put into separate bedrooms.

Another joy was the motor launch, seldom used except at weekends, but we travelled sometimes as far as Gloucester negotiating various lock gates which of course were all worked by hand and necessitated long delays while the lock-keeper sweated at his job. (I used to have many photographs of these excursions, the females with splendid hats and parasols, the men in flannels and boaters, but they were all destroyed in World War II.)

I must tell you something more about my father: he was very volatile, what amused him today, infuriated him tomorrow, which made life rather difficult. He was generous and had enormous charm but a violent temper. When we were very naughty he would send us to bed and stand at the foot of the staircase cracking his horse whip. Of course we knew that Mother would never allow him to touch us, but we acted up splendidly, continuing to weep and wail over a suitable period, until we felt it was safe to take out a book and read. We both read avidly but I can never remember being taught how to do this. In fact I don't remember much of what we were taught but somehow we must have learned to write and we certainly spoke with a pretty French accent.

We had endless governesses. My London cousins had first-rate governesses because of course they had the fun of London where they could spend their free time. We had the dregs because our house was miles from everywhere, and the nearest little town was Berkeley. So there was absolutely nothing for them to do; I presume they spent their off time flirting with the groom or the gardener. I don't know. But they didn't stay long and they taught us little!

So now 1911 loomed and the end of our first decade. I hope I've given a truthful impression of a spoilt, lazy, fat, fiery-tempered brat, because that was what I was. My only asset lay in my genes over which of course I've never had any control, and these produced a keen interest in all things and people, a vivid imagination, flaxen curls and pink and white skin, a retentive memory and, I'm afraid, the fateful Hodder charm, though I didn't know that word then nor did I discover for many, many years that I had it.

In 1912, my father decided that we must be educated – we were extremely unruly – and so we must move to Bristol. He also wanted to move to Bristol from a business point of view because by then he had opened another office in Avonmouth. To get from Berkeley Road to Bristol was effort enough but to run another big office in Avonmouth was almost impossible, so he needed to move as well. Now this strange hiatus occurs in my memories because we must have been an enormous procession – parents, horses, staff, children – all going to Bristol and yet I remember absolutely nothing about it. I suppose I was in one of my emotional moods and was just crying my heart out because I didn't want to leave my lovely home.

Act 1, Scene 1: The Move to Bristol

So I remember nothing of our move from Middleton. Anyhow we reached Bristol and because our new home needed much alteration and decoration we moved first into a house in Downs Park West, a detestable characterless house with a very small garden, but with the Downs freely available for us to play on.

I learned later that my parents had considered two houses, one on the Promenade which is the loveliest of the many lovely roads in Clifton, as well as No.5 Apsley Road.

Then, as now, there were planning restrictions and Daddy couldn't get permission to build a garage in addition to the existing stables. There was a garage and stable belonging to No.5, but this was a property away from the house in a lane just off Whiteladies Road, connected by private telephone. (Many years later when my father had built a garage in the garden at Apsley Road, this property was bought by a large taxi firm.) My father installed central heating, then almost unknown, put a bathroom and lavatory on every floor and had the entire ground floor parqueted. He also reinforced the top floor because he wanted to install a full-size billiard table there.

It was lucky for John and for me that we started school in a small place at the far end of Downs Park. It was run by a charming couple called Mr and Mrs. Milani; he was very musical and played the violin and often, as John and I were walking home, we would stop outside his open window, listening entranced. I can't remember learning anything there except for our music lessons and our dancing, but I think we were happy enough.

My father now had one of his sudden changes of mood and decided that we should no longer be babies but we must grow up and instead of saying Mummy and Daddy, we must say Mother and Father. This was quite strange as our cousins were all allowed to stick to the old custom and indeed continued to call or refer to their parents as Mummy and Daddy in later life.

Another innovation was pocket money. At 10 o'clock on a Saturday morning, we were given the princely sum of half a crown and at once we rushed to the Henleaze shops where we immediately spent the lot. But whereas I returned always with some 'thing', often as not a garish glass bead necklace, which I gave to my poor mother and expected her to wear, John returned with nothing.

I have only two or three pleasant remembrances of that Henleaze period. The first was that my mother's birthday fell in June so we could rush out on to the Downs and pick great armfuls of what we called 'moon daisies', returning to decorate her chair before we all sat down to breakfast. The other happiness was our meeting with the Stanley Allens who lived on the opposite side of the road. Mrs. Allen was a delightful woman; she was a county player who taught us to play tennis. I became great friends with their elegant and accomplished daughter, Joan, and of course we knew both their sons, Hugh and Douglas.

This interlude in Downs Park West was a period of unmitigated disaster. My father had a serious accident, the car was a write-off and he collapsed with pneumonia. John had pneumonia a second time and this time the doctor said he must have a year outside, perhaps on a farm. As at this time my father had a small fishing smack which he kept moored off Sidmouth, our parents felt it would be much better to send John down there to recuperate with the boat's skipper, a fascinating Devon fisherman called Jack and his lovely warm-hearted wife. So John spent the entire winter with them and returned in excellent health with us after we had spent a family Easter holiday there. During this holiday I was taken night fishing for conger eels, a most uncomfortable adventure with a couple of these hideously fierce creatures writhing in the bottom of a small rowing boat. At this time I developed an ear infection, and I shall never forget the agony. In the end I had an operation for mastoid, the first time this operation had been performed outside London. For months afterwards I had to wear bandages or a bonnet because the wound had to be kept open with a tube. As a result I've always been slightly deaf in my left ear.

Then in July 1914 we finally moved into 5 Apsley Road and Grannie Hodder, taken on a tour of inspection, stood at the bottom of the steps and said "I am not enamoured of it". This very pompous remark made us all burst out laughing – to her annoyance – and for many weeks afterwards it became a family catch-phrase. By this time most of the family had moved to Bristol. Lallie lived at the White House in Raleigh Road, my other Hodder aunt, Elfrida, called Freda for short, had recently lost her husband, William Knapman, good-looking and auburn- haired, and so she came from Exeter with her only child, Hugh William Hartly Knapman, to share a house with her widowed mother. As they both disliked each other, the atmosphere must have been a most unhappy one. So at a very early age my father became the *pater familias*.

While we are on the subject of names, there was yet another change. As Hodders we were known throughout much of Gloucestershire, but when we reached Bristol we were constantly asked if we were relations of Hodder the Chemist. So my father decided that we would use his second name, as well as the Hodder, and that's how we became Hartly Hodder – with no 'e' in Hartly and no hyphen, please.

Number 5 was a house we immediately loved. It was spacious, with a reasonably sized garden. Three things we found particularly fascinating: first, the butler's lift which ran from the basement to the butler's pantry, we used this until we moved in 1976. Subsequent small children enjoyed pulling it up and down with a great clatter as much as we had. The second was the private telephone which stood at the top of the basement stairs and which connected only to the garage and stable in Boyce's Avenue. So whenever we needed a car or a horse we turned the handle and spoke. It wasn't the telephone which was new, because we'd always had one, but it was the excitement and pride to think that this one was ours and only ours. Of course when my father sold the garage, the telephone was dismantled.

The third innovation was the row of bells which were slung along the kitchen wall. A bell would jangle fiercely whenever we needed attention from the staff. There were nine bells and each was attached to the main rooms. In the library, drawing room and dining room there were very pretty Victorian painted bell handles, whereas in the main bedrooms and the billiard room embroidered bell ropes hung down the walls. Later relays of children to whom servants and bells were unknown would try the handle in the drawing room and rush downstairs to see if the bell there was still jangling.

Our lives during that month of July were very happy. We noticed how our elegant mother, dressed in the latest Paris fashion, would always go upstairs at 12.30 to put on gloves and hat; this was for lunch, even when we were only *en famille*. There was a great ritual for her in the afternoon: a silver salver was put out on the dresser in the hall and on this any caller would leave visiting cards, one for the wife and two for the husband, unless this particular afternoon was mother's 'at home' day when all visitors would be shown into the drawing room where cucumber sandwiches and tiny cakes would be served. Visitors were expected to stay for only half an hour, so there was a constant to-ing and fro-ing in the hall. When it was

20

not an 'at home', mother would be out leaving cards at the houses of her friends and, if new people came into the district, they were called on within the month, which was an excellent way of welcoming new blood. At that time all the buildings in Apsley Road were houses and we knew all the families inhabiting them until about 1930 when, as times grew hard, landlords started to turn houses into flats and the neighbourhood gradually changed.

We were still inhabiting the school room at this time and were encouraged to come down for tea only when family and friends were there as opposed to new acquaintances. After tea my mother continued her habit of reading to us until we were packed off to bed about 7 p.m. It was really exciting when father returned early, giving us the usual romp. This seldom happened as we now enjoyed what was called 'open house' and he preferred to ring up from his club, the Conservative Constitutional Club of course, to tell my mother how many guests he would be bringing back for dinner. I can't imagine how our poor cook coped, but she was devoted to us all and I'm sure she never grumbled. Even an ordinary dinner consisted of four or five courses and, of course, for a party there would be twelve or even more. Everyone dressed for dinner, a habit which persisted with the Hartly Hodders until 1940.

We had a largish staff: nanny, cook, kitchen maid, two housemaids, a parlour maid, a groom, who doubled as a gardener, a chauffeur who valeted for my father, a sewing maid and two daily maids. Only nanny and the parlour maid slept in the house; the groom slept in the flat above the stable, the chauffeur in the flat above the garage; everyone else came in daily.

There was a firm timetable of household duties: Monday – laundry; Tuesday – ironing; Wednesday – a room would be turned out, almost spring cleaned, as all the furniture would be polished and the walls brushed down; Thursday – the brass would be done: as there were seventy stairs from the hall to the billiard room and each stair had a splendid brass stair rod, as well as the coal scuttles and fenders in most of the rooms, this must have been a tremendous job; Friday – all the silver.

I remember many details about the house. There was a refectory table in the dining room where we could sit eighteen people comfortably and twenty uncomfortably. The drawing room was divided from the library by a sliding door which meant that it gave a wonderful space for large parties and dances, and later provided me with a home-made stage and auditorium when I began my theatrical career in 1916.

The basement was huge. There was a stone scullery with a big basin and a boiler in the opposite corner. Later my father put in a gas cooker, but until that time the cook used the vast iron range in the kitchen. There was another room which was called the staff sitting room, a store cupboard, a coal cellar, where we could store ten tons of coal, a wine cellar, where we could store I don't know how many pipes of port, for father was a great port expert.

On the first floor was the family bathroom and 'loo', my parents' bedroom and dressing room with a basin, my bedroom, the main guest room with en-suite bathroom and 'loo', a second guest room with washbasin, and an airing cupboard. On the first half landing of the top floor was another bathroom and 'loo', and on the top floor was the billiard room and John's bedroom, along with accommodation for Nanny and the parlourmaid, and the housemaid's kitchen which contained a big sink and a gas cooker. In addition, there was a large box room and above it all a loft which extended the length and breadth of the house.

And so we come to August 3rd, 1914, the date fixed by my parents for the official house-warming dinner. In those days, sherry, or perhaps it was Madeira, was served in the library, and when the great brass gong resounded through the house, the guests formed a crocodile – my mother with the most important male guest led the way to the dining room and each couple followed, with my father and the chief female guest bringing up the rear. As of course Nanny had been pressed into service for this event, John and I were left unsupervised and were glued to the staircase watching the proceedings entranced. As my father left the library we heard his voice booming out "Let us eat, drink and be merry for tomorrow we die". Appalling words! We questioned what dying meant and we went miserably to bed, but we couldn't sleep – still, it couldn't be too dreadful as gales of laughter reached us far into the night.

And so the next fateful day dawned – August 4th, 1914. It seemed like any other day to us, for little changed. At first father put up a war map on the library wall and for a few days little flags marked the forward advance of the allied armies. This was soon forgotten as the Germans then pressed ahead, and anyhow the thought of school obsessed us: John was to go as a boarder to Clifton College Pre – and I had been entered for Clifton High School.

"And so to school went she," to misquote Housman. How I detested it! I had been utterly spoilt and was completely unprepared for this structured life. Accustomed to the elegant clothes of my immediate family, I at once hated the frumpish garments worn by most of the teachers. They all seemed so old. My uniform was detestable, white blouse, scratchy navy blue gym slip, woollen stockings. Mother, surveying me sadly on my first day, decided that a blue bow on top of my curls would be an improvement but alas, at morning prayers, Miss Phillips, the headmistress, took it upon herself to remark on the ostentation of some people who strive to look different. As no one else looked different in any way, every eye in the hall sought out my blue bow, so of course I didn't wear that again.

I hated Miss Phillips and, being idle and bored, was a nuisance to all and there were frequently – indeed there were always – remarks like "Eileen has not yet learned to keep the silence rule" on every report. Then at last came a younger teacher wearing a bottle green skirt, quite short, and lisle stockings. She taught History, and for the first time my interest was captured and History became one of the subjects to fascinate me all my life. I was still stupid and idle and could conceal a French or German text book in my hymn book and would learn a few relevant facts while ostensibly singing the hymns.

As the years dragged on things went from bad to worse, so I started to write notes to my next door neighbour and before long we had a regular correspondence. In one note she asked if I'd ever been kissed by a boy. "Of course," I replied. "Where?" she asked. "Everywhere," wrote I. "Not your fanny?" At this point the long-suffering teacher pounced on us both and seized the offending scraps of paper. These were of course sent to Miss Phillips who was rightly appalled and suspended us from school, while the Council debated our fate.

It was easily established that I couldn't have had any contact with the opposite sex because every moment of my day could be accounted for. So I was allowed to return but I had my desk placed in front and well away from the rest of the class so that I couldn't contaminate them with my unhealthy mind. Most of my class kindly ignored the whole episode but strangely enough the unhealthy minds of the form above were keenly interested and they took to inviting me out to tea where I speedily learnt some of the facts of life as interpreted by ill-informed 14- and 15-year olds.

I can now refer to my first scrap book where I begin to see the names of friends, the Riseleys, the Shirleys, Betty Shove, Nancy Tricks, Phyllis Smale, Marion Pope, the Swains, the Bouchers, Nancye Steadman and Peggy Wood. All were involved in our dancing displays and theatrical productions which were given for charity, usually in aid of the soldiers. By 1915/16 Mother in her Women's Voluntary Aid uniform, and her friends, were organising riverside parties for the wounded, who all wore shapeless blue flannel jackets and trousers. The men were ferried out there by car and the stronger rowed up and down the river, while the rest sat about and were given a scrumptious tea.

A concert would follow. This was when I was first asked to 'recite' and I chose 'Barbara Fritchie', a poem about an old grey-haired woman clutching a flag as rebel soldiers approached her. "'Shoot if you must this old grey head but spare your country's flag,' she said." About the most unsuitable lines any 14 year-old flaxen curled child could have spoken, but I'm told it brought tears to the eyes of the most hardened listener. I must have been a 'pot hunter' in those days, for I also used it to win my first Bronze medal at the Bristol Eisteddfod.

Things now began to improve at school. My English teacher was a Miss Arbuthnot-Lane, sister of a well-known London surgeon. She was a woman of wide knowledge and taste and she soon discovered that I was enthralled by words, so she encouraged me to read widely. When I did well in what was then called Lower Certificate with first grades in English and History, she began to suggest that I would be suitable for Oxford where she had studied. The High School also put on their first pupils' show, *Iolanthe*, a brilliant satire by Gilbert and Sullivan, in which I sang the part of Phyllis.

All these activities encouraged me to write my own shows. Pantomimes, naturally, in which all the family were involved, even my father, who maddened me because he wouldn't learn his lines. Every Sunday afternoon from September we would rehearse in the billiard room for a couple of hours. Of course I played the lovely princess and the rest of the cast had to say wonderful things about me! When lines were learnt and 'business' worked out, we would descend to the drawing room for further work with mother at the piano. I designed programmes, costumes, the lot, and we presented the shows using the library as our stage, while the audience, who paid a shilling for programmes – and there was a silver collection after-wards – sat in the drawing room.

By this time at school I was moving into Higher Certificate with the idea of going to Oxford. I should tell you that I've always been idiotic at Maths, I still can't add up my bridge scores without using my fingers, and as Maths is a must for any good university, my father arranged for me to be coached by an ex-Army officer in College Road. He was a dear with a beautiful garden. I suppose he realised at once that I was a hopeless case for after the first couple of lessons he didn't bother any more but took me around the garden picking choice posies and succulent fruit for me. The net result was that I passed English, French and History with first grades but failed Maths abysmally.

Miss Lane thought she could use her influence to get me into St. Hugh's regardless, so up we went to Oxford which I adored, but when we reached St. Hugh's I disliked the strict atmosphere and dowdy appearance of most of the undergraduates. At this point my father intervened – he had never cared for the Oxford idea – and now floated the thought of a finishing school in Paris, which sounded far more fun.

But life was already more exciting because I had attracted the attention of an officer complete with a batman and brilliantly polished riding boots, who later came up every Sunday from Sandhurst on a magnificent motor cycle. All my friends had admirers by this time but they were rather spotty boys from Clifton College – and I had a real live man. My father didn't approve at all of this new development and used all his persuasive powers for the Paris project. He tried to bribe me in all sorts of ways. One was to give me my own bank account. Mr. Houslander, the genial manager of the Corn Street branch of the Midland Bank, had a special tiny cheque book enclosed in a small white leather case made for me and Midland have kept me in white leather cases ever since.

But now 1918 was upon us and the end of World War I. During those four years, the war had impinged only slightly upon me, a deliberate strategy on the part of my parents. True there had been signs, first the horses went, then the groom, then slowly everyone on the staff was conscripted until we were left only with Nanny, who became cook and general factotum. But I was always kept so busy with my activities and, as Nanny always fed me well, there was no reason why I should concern myself with the outside world.

Now, however, father had one of his sudden changes of mood; he decided that John and I should be made aware of this dreadful catastrophe in the hope that we would never permit it to happen again. So he hired a black London taxi cab and Cockney driver and off we went among the very first people allowed on to the battlefields. Never shall I forget the horror of the next three days as we drove through miles of desolation, roofless dwellings, stricken trees blackly outlined against a cold sky. We stayed in hotels with only tarpaulins to keep out the cold. On the third day, our driver said we could get out as all shells had been removed, so out we got gingerly, and began to move towards the first trench, but almost immediately my mother called out – she had kicked a gangrenous leg in a torn German jackboot. We turned and fled for the coast.

Slowly the picture of my life changed again. A smaller staff returned to Apsley Road. I was given a car and my first dress allowance and horrified Mother by buying a backless black satin evening gown – before I had always worn only pink, white and blue. Horses came back and I was sent for riding lessons to another ex-Army officer who made me ride and jump stirrup-less and saddle-less. He discovered that I had a slight curvature of the spine and I had to endure the most unpleasant treatment – cold water sponged on my back, a daily hour lying flat on a board, and frequent instructions to stand straight. I must admit that all this was very beneficial for I still stand and sit straight.

The war years had taken a dreadful toll of my parents' lives, both had overworked and both now suffered a nervous breakdown. Father became more choleric and unpredictable than ever, but mother lost her voice completely and could only whisper for two years.

But now Paris loomed and again I fought against the parental decision for by now Michael Stotesbury and I had fallen in love and we wanted to get married. Alan Marcus Stotesbury (known as Michael) fell in love with me when I was a schoolgirl of 16; he was serving during the last weeks of the 1914–1918 war, at the end of which he resigned his commission to join his father's Bristol engineering firm. Father was still resolutely opposed to the idea, rightly I think now, although I didn't then. I was certainly much too young and Michael was a penniless Regular Army Lieutenant, so the outlook wasn't bright. Of course father won and off I went to Madame Manileve's Finishing School in Auteuil near the Longchamps racecourse.

Act I, Scene 2: Paris 1920–1921

All this time Michael and I had exchanged passionate love letters and I was still longing to marry him, but it was now time to prepare for Paris in September and eventually I arrived at Madame Manileve's Finishing School. I was dreadfully homesick and wept ceaselessly for the first few days until, on the Saturday night, a few of us were taken to the Comédie Française where I saw a wonderful production of *Cyrano de Bergerac*. His final words, 'mon panache', untranslatable into English, still ring in my ears and years later I used the expression quite frequently to indicate special pleasure when I had to judge a play. So by the time I returned to Auteuil that evening the tears were replaced with smiles and I determined to enjoy what turned out to be one of the most satisfying and exciting years of my life.

The school was in a delightful house with a large garden. I had a bedroom at the top of the house with a bathroom on the same floor. This wasn't en suite but no one else seemed to have the desire to bath every day, so I came to look upon it as mine. We worked very hard, we studied music, dancing, singing and French, we visited all the art galleries and museums where we had lectures on the important artists from our own brilliant French professor, M de la Fontaine. (Of course we called him Pierre Lapin.) We learned to cook with Mademoiselle Briand, another member of staff. I was stupid enough to ask to be excused from these lessons as I preferred to have extra French lessons. Mademoiselle was a splendid cook and our meals were always delicious. When I left she gave me a French cookery book so for many years we enjoyed exciting dishes like Oeuf à la Neige, Nègre en Chemise – no longer politically correct, I suppose – and Tripe à la Mode de Caen.

There were only three rules in the house, punctuality for meals and classes, essays to be handed in every morning and no English to be spoken among ourselves. We all kept these rules faithfully. There were three churches available, Protestant, Catholic and Jewish. I toyed with the idea of Catholicism but though I enjoyed the service I disliked the strident colours of the saints, but, as a matter of fact I was already becoming an agnostic, and after a few visits, I ceased my religious attendances.

I adored Paris, life was most enjoyable, we rode, played tennis, often had small dances, 'hops' really, accompanied by a gramophone or occasionally the piano. We were very carefully chaperoned and the young Frenchmen had to return us to Madame Manileve's care whenever the music stopped. We went occasionally to the races, we explored Versailles and Fontaine-bleau. My fellow students were a very agreeable bunch. They came mostly from London and we all frequently visited each other when we returned to England – happy friendships which lasted up to World War II when everything changed so dramatically.

There was another visiting staff called Yvonne Keeble, the only child of a famous Oxford professor and scientist, Sir Frederick Keeble. She and I struck up a great friendship although she was much older than I. We often went shopping together – Paris shops are 'ravissants' – and as she was very extravagant and I had never learned to manage my money I amassed a considerable and very lovely wardrobe every bit of which, from knickers to jackets, was hand made and hand embroidered.

Concerning which, I remember an incident while walking along the rue de Rivoli. My knickers suddenly fell down; dreadfully embarrassed I stepped out of them and went on my way when suddenly a male voice shouted, "Mademoiselle, Mademoiselle, vous avez laisser tomber vos pantalons" and a very attractive young man rushed up and handed me the offending garment! I must tell you that earlier my father had forgotten to open an account for me in Paris, so with my last sou I sent a telegram – "funds urgently needed". Incidentally, I was in France when Marlene Dietrich was ordered off the streets of Paris by the police because she was wearing a man's jacket and trousers!

(Many years later I saw her perform at Bristol Hippodrome, having of course heard her sing endless times on radio during the intervening years, for she was the idol of both the German and British forces. On the occasion in Bristol she spent the entire day working with her electricians in order to get the lighting exactly focused on her in order to accentuate her beauty. That night she wore a magnificent glittering skin-tight creation with a mink train that disappeared into the wings. During the thundering applause after each song, she would walk slowly off stage giving a final tweak to this train so the stage was bare! Each time she returned we all hurled fresh pink roses and carnations until every inch was carpeted and there she stood enveloped in this flattering perfumed colour – no wonder the young males leapt over the footlights and bore her triumphantly shoulder high through the stalls out on to the Centre and then propelled her waiting car through the city to her hotel.)

By this time it was 1921. John had left Clifton College. My mother wished him to go to Oxford to follow in the footsteps of Grandpapa Baron, but it was finally decided to send him to France and Germany to prepare him for a business career in shipping, so off he went to Le Havre to join a firm in which father had an interest. For our first Easter holiday in France we decided to explore Brittany. Yvonne joined us, luckily too, for few Bretons could speak French and we should have been hopelessly at sea without her. One day we reached Point du Raz and gazing helplessly at the raging sea beneath I discovered that I suffered from vertigo; there was no turning back and our guide dragged me, an inert sack, to the other side.

Then back to Paris for the last happy term and for the summer vacation father took a house in Etretat, a largish village not all that far from Deauville where we frequently gambled. We kept the 'yacht' moored in the harbour and John and I took the dinghy and explored every nook and cranny of the coast, an enterprise which was to serve him well during World War II when as a member of the splendid 'little ships' he and his friends assailed the German Navy month after month.

So this happiest of years came to an end, but it was not really an end because for years I revisited Paris, spent weekends and holidays there with my fellow students and attended all Manileve's London reunions.

Naturally I had told everyone of my love affair with Michael and that we expected to get married as soon as I returned home. But Father had other ideas. He refused even to announce my engagement. So Michael and I decided that we would tell our nearest and dearest that we had got married. This was easily achieved by the simple device of buying a plain gold ring which I wore on the correct finger and for the next year or so we spent constant long 'honeymoons' with our long-suffering friends, sometimes in London, sometimes in Kingskerswell, a little village outside Torquay where Joy, only daughter of Clara Butt and Kennerley Rumford, and I stayed with friends.

29

Act I, Scene 3: The Twenties – and Marriage

It was strange after the independence of the previous two years to find myself back at Apsley Road, only to realise that Betty Shove was also in residence there and strangely was calling my parents, Mother and Father. I resented this but tried to understand that the orphaned girl had found shelter and love with my ever-generous family. Of course I plunged into the social whirl of Clifton life. My immediate circle consisted of Joyce Boucher, Betty of course, Nancye Steadman, the Wills, the three Stotesbury men and the three Wansbroughs. These last two families had the wonderful good luck to welcome all their sons back from the war, while so many of our friends had lost theirs.

Having danced at balls in Bristol and Bath, hunt balls all winter, exciting ones in London, Oxford and Cambridge in the summer, endless private dances, tea dances on Saturday afternoons at the Berkeley Café in Bristol and the Berkeley Hotel in London, I adored it all, especially the waltz and the tango. I remember one amusing incident at a New College Ball in Oxford, some bright spark – could it have been Maurice Bowra? – decided to invent a new language by adding another syllable to every final consonant, so waste paper basket became wagga pagga bagga and the Prince of Wales, then everyone's heart-throb, the Pagga Wagga, so of course the rest of us spent the evening inventing new words. By the next day every Oxford college was employing the device, by the day after it had reached the town, by the end of the week it flourished throughout England, whereupon Oxford immediately dropped it – and the ridiculous invention has never been heard of again, unlike Oxford bags which filthily swept every quad for about two years.

Everyone played tennis throughout the summer – in those days it was a kind of 'pat ball' requiring no run back and no female served overarm. In the winter we all rode; we no longer had our own horses but were content to hire and gallop over the Downs or at Kingsweston, hunting from time to time with the Berkeley. A great friend of father's, Henry Hosegood who lived in Minehead, persuaded him that we ought to try stag hunting, so down we went to a splendid Meet at Cloutsham and found the stag almost immediately. He gave us a wonderful run all day. I was unaccustomed to this kind of country and was unceremoniously unseated when my horse plunged through a thicket; no one had told me that I must lie towards his tail, so of course I bent forward towards his neck and was entangled, like Absolom, in the thorns as the horse went forward. On we went towards the Doone Valley, and there high above us outlined against the scarlet sunset stood this magnificent creature who had outwitted us all. But, alas, the Master, Sir Denis Boles, ordered him to be lassoed and he was thrown to the hounds.

Burning with rage, I rode up to Sir Denis and attacked him fiercely. Then I turned and rode away into the night but before too long I was terrified as I realised that I was riding a strange horse in unknown country, but fortunately for me the animal knew his way and finally delivered me to his Minehead stable just as my worried host was about to organise a search party. After that I never hunted again.

Strangely enough I'm always ambivalent about the sport, to see and hear hounds streaming across the countryside stirs me still, so whenever I am with devoted hunters I oppose them strongly and when I am surrounded by anti-hunters I stand up for the activity. After all, as a good countrywoman, I know only too well the havoc any fox can cause to lamb and fowl, and yet I rejoice when I look from my town window and see a magnificent dog fox sitting on my lawn.

This was the time when actors and actresses were really great, such names as Matheson Lang, Beatrice Lillie, the Lunts, Ralph Lynn, Martin Harvey, Ivor Novello, George Robey, Paul Robeson, spring to mind. So it was little wonder that I returned one evening to dinner and announced that I had decided to have a career: I would train as an actress. That caused a huge row. My infuriated father said "Never!", so I swept from the room and early next morning telephoned Mr. Houslander to ask him to put £300 ready for me as I was travelling immediately to London. He replied, "Dear girl, your father has just beaten you, he has closed your account." Within twenty four hours I had ascertained that the training for an actress and for a drama teacher was basically the same; I also found that I had a friend with a vacancy for a French teacher in his prep. school, so, with the money I earned teaching French, I paid for my drama course, only it was called 'elocution' in those days.

So now I worked all day and danced most of the night, house parties at weekends were 'de rigueur', we met for dinner on Fridays and left on Monday mornings, and a splendid time was had by all. I was the first of family and friends to attain the age of twenty one, then a really important milestone in one's life. My mother presented me at Court just prior to my birthday; she wore a beautiful Worth creation in black panne velvet and I wore a white hand-embroidered sequinned gown so heavy that I found it quite difficult to keep curtseying. It was exciting to drive slowly down The Mall with people commenting as one passed: only John disapproved of my appearance. When he saw me at the top of the staircase he said I looked like the fairy on top of the Christmas tree in a pantomime. I wore this same creation for my 21st birthday when I received the most wonderful gifts.

None of the family attended the Court presentation except my mother and me, just the two of us coming down The Mall. We disembarked at the entrance to Buckingham Palace and were escorted to the Throne Room. The Royal Family sat in a semi-circle with the Queen and King of course in the middle. Your sponsor would come forward to say "I'd like to propose that my daughter (or my niece or whoever it was) be accepted at Court." She would then step back and you would come forward and curtsey to each of the people in the semi-circle in turn – about fourteen I think in my semi-circle. All the Royal Family can be there, you see.

The following weekend I was to spend with friends, the Olives, outside Bristol, so stupidly I took most of my birthday possessions to show them off. The chauffeur drove me down on Friday night and John came to fetch me on the Monday. He strapped my beautiful crocodile gold-plated suitcase on to the luggage rack but carelessly failed to put the strap through the handle – when we reached Apsley Road, the suitcase had vanished, never to be seen again. Our insurance didn't cover the loss, so I never again possessed so many exquisite things.

Father had promised to announce my engagement to Michael at supper time, but to my anger he failed to keep his promise, fuelling even more strongly our growing antagonism.

By 1922 I had passed my LGSM and LRAM and had to look for work. I realised that Aunt Lallie Hicks had a full quota of staff with Phyllis Smale and Margaret Davies in her drama school, so I searched the education columns in the local press and found an advertisement for a post in Taunton. On impulse, I leapt into a train and presented myself at Weirfield School. There were joint principals, one fat, Miss Murray, a good pianist but utterly lacking either in charm or musicianship; the other, Miss Jenkin, tall and thin with a keen interest in the arts. They accepted me and I started there in the September with two pupils from the school, Joan Stephenson and Betty Culliford, and one outside student, Molly Hancock. Mrs. Hancock alarmed

WEDDING AT ST. MARY REDCLIFF.

Stotesbury—Hartly-Hodder.

The wedding of Mr Alan Marcus Stotesbury, youngest son of Colonel and Mrs Stotesbury, and Miss Eileen Edith Hartly-Hodder, only daughter of Councillor C. Hartly-Hodder and Mrs C. Hartly-Hodder, took place at St. Mary Redcliff Church on Saturday. The officiating clergy were the Rev. Canon W. Welchman and the Rev. Canon Bateman-Champain.

The bride, who was given away by her father, wore a dress of ivory georgette, with antique lace, the gift of the bride's uncle, Sir Mortimer Singer, and a lace train lined with mauve georgette. The lace veil was lent by the bride's mother. The bride also wore a head-dress of orange blossom and silver, and carried a bouquet of lilies of the valley.

The bridesmaids were the Misses Joan Allen, Sheila Langdon Down, Peggie Hodge, Elizabeth C. Shove, Nancy St. John Hickman and Telma Waldron. They wore mauve chiffon velvet with underskirts of silver lace, black felt and velvet hats, with amethyst ornament, and carried bouquets of lilac—the two latter items the gift of the bridegroom. The best man was Mr Gilbert Dyke Wansbrough, and the groomsmen were Messrs Adrian Bowring, J. Hartly-Hodder (brother of the bride), Capt. T. R. A. Morris, and Messrs Kenneth Kingham and L. J. Stotesbury (brother of the bridegroom).

There was a large congregation, which included the Lord Mayor and Lady Mayoress, at the church. While the congregation were assembling the organist (Mr Ralph T. Morgan) played Mendelssohn's Second Sonata, Cantilene (Wolstenholme), Marche Nuptiale (Guilmant), and the introduction to the third act and Bridal March from " Lohengrin." The hymns, " Praise my soul, the King of Heaven," " O Perfect love, all human thought transcending." " May the Grace of Christ our Saviour," and Psalm 67 were sung, and during the signing of the register the choir sang Sir Fredk. Bridges' " Sweeter than Songs of Summer," Mendelssohn's Wedding March being played as the bride and bridegroom left the church.

The honeymoon is to be spent in Paris. The bride's travelling dress was of reseda green crêpe-de-chine, with accordion-pleated godets, and trimmed with dull gold embroidery. She wore a coat of face cloth to match and a soft green straw hat. A largely attended reception was held at the home of the bride, 5, Apsley Road.

MR ALAN STOTESBURY AND MISS EILEEN HARTLY-HODDER.

The wedding of Mr Alan Marcus Stotesbury, youngest son of Colonel and Mrs Stotesbury, with Miss Eileen Edith Hartly-Hodder, only daughter of Councillor C. Hartly-Hodder and Mrs C. Hartly-Hodder, took place at St. Mary Redcliff Church, this afternoon. The officiating clergy were the Rev. Canon W. Welchman and the Rev. Canon Bateman-Champain.

The bride, who was given away by her father, wore a dress of ivory georgette, with antique lace, the gift of the bride's uncle, Sir Mortimer Singer, and a lace train lined with mauve georgette. The lace veil was lent by the bride's mother. The bride also wore a head-dress of orange blossom and silver, and carried a bouquet of lilies of the valley.

The bridesmaids were the Misses Joan Allen, Sheila Langdon Down, Peggie Hodge, Elizabeth C. Shove, Nancy St. John Hickman and Telma Waldron. They wore mauve chiffon velvet with underskirts of silver lace, black felt and velvet hats, with amethyst ornament, and carried a bouquet of lilac—the two latter items the gift of the bridegroom. The best man was Mr Gilbert Dyke Wansbrough, and the groomsmen were Messrs Adrian Bowring, J. Hartly-Hodder (brother of the bride), Capt. T. R. A. Morris, Kenneth Kingham and L. J. Stotesbury (brother of bridegroom).

The honeymoon is to be spent in Paris. The bride's travelling dress was of reseda green crêpe-de-chine, with accordion-pleated godets, and trimmed with dull gold embroidery. She wore a coat of face cloth to match and a soft green straw hat. A largely attended reception was held at the home of the bride, 5, Apsley Road.

Eileen's wedding to Michael Stotesbury was widely recorded in the national and local press.

33

me at our first meeting by telling me that her daughter, aged 24, was rather young and lacking in confidence. As I was only 21 I was very uncertain about tackling the young woman but we soon became great friends. I loved teaching from the first and the children warmed to me. By the end of the first year I had a great many pupils on my list and by 1923 I had so many Guildhall examination successes that dear Dan Roberts recommended me to take an acting course with the Scottish Community Drama Association.

My parents were busy, too. By 1924 father had been adopted as Councillor for Clifton North Ward, and was also President of the Chamber of Commerce, while mother was founding the first branch of the Women's National Lifeboat Association in Bristol. She organised flag days for the whole of Bristol. Mother and I travelled hundreds of miles delivering boxes, these were counted by volunteers from the various Queen Square shipping and grain offices at the Canadian and White Sea Building by courtesy of dear Mr. Ray, the manager there. Several years previously all the family joined the Bristol Playgoers Club, so with all this and political work, plus our entertaining, we were an extremely busy household. Mother and her friend Vera Saville founded the first Women's Conservative Luncheon Club in Bristol and so life was exciting and full.

But now more dangerous topics pervaded the political scene. Bernard Shaw's voice was heard on the wireless, we began to hear of Socialism, of the Fabian Society, of Margaret Bondfield, who became the first woman cabinet minister, widows received their first pensions. The Zinoviev letter scandal caused the collapse of the minority Labour Government of Ramsay Macdonald; and Stanley Baldwin was returned with a large Conservative majority.

Then came the miners' strike and father's mine, the Princess Royal Colliery in the Forest of Dean, had to close due to flooding, causing a temporary financial crisis in the Hodder household, only surmounted because my mother sold many shares. Father even borrowed the £500 given earlier to John and me by my godmother, this action causing much trouble later because father always denied that he had received the money. All this was followed by the General Strike in 1926 when the nation was paralysed for a week. John and Michael played their part in breaking the strike – Michael on the trains and John in the docks.

Nevertheless, I progressed steadily with my career and now decided that I would become a solo performer. I think this was inspired by that wonderful American actress Ruth Draper, who with the smallest change of hat or cloak could people the stage with every kind of character. Of course we all decided we could write our own material. I was fairly successful in this with one monologue published by French, while several were used by the BBC. A certain Frederick Piffard, later killed by a lion in foreign parts, took a great fancy to me and my work and I had a splendid life during the short time of his dominance. Alas, one Francis Worsley rightly disapproved of our friendship and both Frederick and I were summarily dismissed.

And now it was 1926 and at last Michael and I got married in St. Mary Redcliffe. It was a huge wedding with some five or six hundred guests, ten bridesmaids and ten ushers. Alas, by this time I realised that I was no longer in love with Michael but I just hadn't the courage to break away, so many people knew of the struggle we had waged since 1918, so many people thought that we were already married, so there it was, a fait accompli, and off we went to Paris for our honeymoon. Of course, we spent all our money there and returned penniless to Southampton. Father's chauffeur and a car met us, it was a bitterly cold day, but we had only enough cash to give the man a coffee and a bun, while we sat hungrily in the car.

I had finally married Michael but alas I was much too young to know my own mind and that year I fell in love with someone else. Michael was a fine man and I treated him abominably.

Act 2, Scene 1: The Thirties – Marriage, Career, Divorce

After the wedding, we returned to our own home, 8 Apsley Road, a large top flat, almost opposite No.5. This just had to happen because the housing situation was still difficult and accommodation hard to find. Most of the flat was furnished with family antiques but I made the dining room rather special. It was art nouveau, black carpet and walls, golden velvet drapes, blue and gold lacquer furniture, tables, chairs and sideboard, with a hanging blue Lalique centre lamp. Its only disadvantage was that it had an outside uncovered staircase so every time I went up and down, remembering my vertigo, I had to keep my eyes fixed and couldn't look down. We had the sweetest little Irish maid – she was paid £2 a week which was the going rate; she was cook, parlourmaid and lady's maid, never have I had a more wonderful member of staff. She was no housemaid and believed in brushing everything under the carpet. But as she liked cleaning silver and polishing the furniture I never fussed about the dust!

Of course, at first we were very happy. Michael enjoyed his rugby, he and my father got on well together and ran all sorts of charities including the Bristol Mons 1914 Star Club. Still there were endless dinner parties, balls, race meetings, nightclubs, the lot, and my autograph album was full of the names of the great and the good of those days: Field Marshal Lord Allenby, cabinet ministers Sir Philip Runciman and Sir Alfred Mond, tennis champions Suzanne Lenglen and William Tilden II, Kreisler, the famous violinist, Sir Frederick Keeble and Lillah McCarthy, Bernard Shaw, Ernie Bevin, the dockers' advocate.

Somehow I had the energy to continue to develop my career, quite apart from producing plays everywhere – in Minehead, Taunton, Bristol – in acting myself, first of all with Edgar Harrison, who later starred in the famous *Archers* radio series, and later with Hedley Goodall and the late Barbara Macrae in Hedley's newly formed Bristol Drama Club.

However, my special interest lay in developing a double act. I would speak the poems and my wonderful raven-haired friend would accompany me on the piano. I have never worked with a more sensitive or knowledgeable musician. If I said "the mood changes here" she would immediately introduce an arpeggio passage perhaps, and if I said "in the next stanza there is a hint of loneliness", she would modulate at once from major to minor.

We met most mornings at ten o'clock either at her house or at mine and would work until lunch time. One morning I expected her as usual but she never came, I telephoned, no reply, I rang her husband's office, he wasn't available. Never again did I see or hear from her; some sixty years later from a common friend I learned that her husband had that morning gone through her drawers and, finding forbidden contraceptives, had met her on the doorstep and banished her immediately from their home. This disruption of our work and friendship was one of the cruellest blows I have ever suffered. I shall never understand why she failed to make some kind of contact with me. The story hurts me dreadfully, even today.

Hedley Goodall and I made history by being invited to go to Cardiff to broadcast a one-act play. Over we went by train and were handed a script, no rehearsal except what we did in a very dark cupboard by ourselves, but anyhow our director seemed pleased and we returned, each clutching a cheque for £5, probably the only performers who have ever been paid promptly by the BBC. Hedley of course went on to a fine career in both radio and television, but it was never my scene. I was poor at dialects and in any case by now had collected around me a band of intelligent and imaginative students. We formed ourselves into a group and, having competed and conquered at Bristol Eisteddfod, we sallied forth to Oxford where the great poets of that time were organising verse speaking contests, including choral speaking, then a very innovative skill.

The judges, poets all, would sit in a semi-circle – John Masefield, Laurence Binyon, the Scottish poet Gordon Bottomley, later to become a great friend, the Sitwells, Walter De la Mare – they were all there while we performed in the hall. We didn't do very well because the judges fancied all the Scottish groups who chanted their Highland poems – a technique well suited to Gaelic, but useless when it was applied to English verse speaking. We returned rather disconsolate to our very old hostelry where we all slept in an annexe and during the night I opened my eyes to be confronted by a cowled ghost kneeling at the side of my bed. Petrified I switched on the light and of course he vanished. When next morning I enquired if the place was haunted, the manager told me that in the 1600s 30 monks had been imprisoned there only to be burned at the stake in the square next morning.

When Michael and I went later to Oxford, we stayed with the Keebles who had a house in Boar's Hill. Among their neighbours were the

Masefields and we often went across after dinner to hear the poet read his works. He always sat in a great armchair in an inglenook, while his wife perched on a stool at his feet. He read beautifully, while she wept continuously. But it was a wonderful experience, especially when we listened to him reading poems like 'Dauber', or more exciting still, 'Reynard the Fox'. I have always enjoyed the latter poem with its brilliant portrayal of hunting types and its understanding of the suffering fox. I have studied many of Masefield's works, he has such a wide range backed by a deep knowledge of the classics. Later on I played Procula in his *Herod* with the well known professional actor, Felix Felton, who was Pilate. While I was in Oxford I was lucky enough to be asked to a concert given by the Sitwells. They sat behind black curtains with only their voices ringing out, a precursor of radio technique.

Then back to Bristol where we were all involved in the Zoo fêtes, at that time one of the highlights of Clifton society. The roundabouts made a merry noise, our male friends in white top hats and long white coats nonchalantly leapt on and off the whirling machines, while in the marquee we girls served wonderful teas which had been prepared by our mamas. All this noise had to cease by 11 o'clock to satisfy the long-suffering Clifton citizens who didn't want go to the fête. Obviously nobody wanted to go home at that hour so we all wandered off to various houses or to a tatty old place which we called a night club but which bore no resemblance whatever to the London night clubs that we knew.

By the way I must tell you about a well know tune which we sang particularly at Mrs. Merrick's which was the most famous of the night clubs: "I danced with a man who danced with a girl who danced with a man who danced with a girl. . . ." and you went on in this idiotic repetition *ad infinitem* until the final line which was "who danced with the Prince of Wales". Anyhow, on that particular night, my immediate party went to Brownie's studio intending to dance out the night.

Brownie was Gladys Methven-Brownlee, daughter of Colonel Methven-Brownlee, a most delightful woman, an amusing rebel, who had taken up photography as a career and this she turned into an art form. She photographed me many times. She lived at the top of the house on the corner of Park Street and Charlotte Street, where she had had cut for her in the wall a huge circular window with a marvellous view out over the city into the hills beyond.

Michael and I arrived there with a couple of friends. I had a new gown for the occasion, a pale pink taffeta (this was a new material which made an enticing frou-frou whenever one moved), a fairly low-cut bodice and bouffant skirt, quite a confection. As we came up the stairs a young man appeared at the top with a lively youngish woman whom I knew. As Shakespeare said, "love is merely a madness" for from that moment Douglas and I fell immediately and utterly in love. His name was Douglas Cleverdon and he owned a bookshop below the studio.

We both behaved disgracefully, we danced the entire evening together, poor Michael was completely at sea and the young woman had hysterics half way through. The following morning after Michael had left for his office, I found this exquisite anonymous poem in my letter box:

> See, see my own sweet jewel
> See what I have here for my darling,
> A robin redbreast and a starling,
> These I give both in hope to woo thee
> and yet thou sayest I do not love thee.

Anyway life went on, work developed, weddings, birthdays, funerals, parties came and went. Michael besought me to think again, my intimate friends begged me to consider the consequences, but nothing could check that passion. Like Mrs. Patrick Campbell, I preferred the "hurly burly of the chaise longue to the chaste comfort of the double bed", only in our case it was the hills and valleys of Somerset that we enjoyed and indeed there we heard the cuckoo on May 11th that year.

Summer came and down Douglas and I went to Cornwall. We went with Brownie and her friend Edith Schwalm. They lived in a caravan and cooked for us and we slept in a small bell tent. The meadow was idyllic, tamarisk-fringed, the sea some twenty feet below, a delightful farmer arrived every morning with eggs, milk and cream. This purposeless leisurely agreeable passing of time describes this wonderful fortnight of perfect weather and safe bathing. My only complaint was the compulsory use of the Elsan in the hedge.

But Saturday came and the hour of departure from bliss to reality. I can't imagine why we never envisaged Michael's reaction to this episode, but we were soon to be enlightened as, before we reached Bridgwater, we realised that we were being followed. At Bridgwater we stopped for a drink at The Clarence. The strange car stopped too. When we restarted, because I knew Bridgwater so well, we swung almost immediately into a right hand turning off the main road, while the following car rushed on its journey, but we knew the game was up and I reached No.8 to find an empty flat, and the next morning divorce papers were served on me.

Now I had to face my family, a dreadful experience because it shocked them so deeply. Divorce was a rare occurrence in those days, although with my rather racketty London friends I'd met a number of cases, but Bristol wasn't London and as the weeks dragged on I soon realised the difference in attitudes. My real friends were absolutely loyal throughout, but a number of acquaintances made their disapproval very clear.

In those days every letter was read out in court and certainly neither Douglas nor I relished this, Douglas especially for he had always insisted that I destroyed all correspondence, but because his letters were so beautiful, so fascinating, I had never done this, so of course it was easy for Michael to ransack my desk in my absence. As I was friendly with the editors of the various local papers, I made appointments to see each one and threw myself on their mercy pointing out correctly that the national press would certainly seize on many of those passages thus causing a scandal that could well wreck my career. The editors all agreed to my request and Friday's columns carried only the briefest of details, thus shielding not only me but my family.

On Saturday I decided that I must face the music at once so I made my usual way to the Berkeley Café where we all habitually met for morning coffee. I bought my usual packet of biscuits and turned with a cheerful 'good morning' to people on the first table only to be ignored completely. This was a dreadful shock, and I could only turn round and walk out.

Most of my friends and all my pupils continued to give me their love and support. In those days, news of any sort took several days to travel, people in Taunton seldom bothered to read Bristol news and when a parent turned up at Weirfield School and informed the principals that one of their staff had been divorced, they immediately telephoned the people with whom I stayed when working late, asking them for further information. My landlady, bless her, said that she knew nothing of the incident and in any case she would always support me whatever I did. I never heard a dicky bird about the matter from anyone else there, a very lucky escape.

At this time in Bristol, Douglas and I talked of marriage but neither of us felt inclined to risk it at once so we continued as lovers in No.8, both of us going our own ways as obviously my family would never countenance our relationship. The simplest way was for us all to ignore the matter. I should like to mention several families who had stuck with me through good times and bad since the 1920s. First there were the Wansbroughs, who lived opposite and who were wonderful in every way. Then there were the Steadmans who gave the most frequent and splendid parties. (I have known the Steadmans since 1918 and am shattered that the last dear member known to me died this Christmas, 1998.) I attended my first garden party there and disgraced myself by accepting Jack Wansbrough's 'dare' that I couldn't eat twelve ice creams during the afternoon. If I won he would give me a dozen pairs of long white kid gloves – of course I won, in spite of the unfair way that Mr. England, the caterer, gradually doubled the size of each helping. I still possess three pairs!

Mrs. Steadman was a Welsh woman, she possessed a lovely portrait of herself in traditional Welsh costume. She had a daughter Nancye and two sons. Nancye was very tall and had a deep voice and was a splendid friend to me, she was always amused to sit beside me and compare the relative sizes of our hands and feet. She loved the theatre and was a good amateur actress; one always knew when Nancye was in the audience because when the laughter died down, suddenly Nancye would appreciate the joke and her 'ho, ho, ho' would ring out in the silence. She had fallen in love with Jack Wansbrough, they made a splendid pair but Jack, alas, was in love with a married woman many years his senior. Jack's younger brother, Gordon, was deeply in love with Nancye but Mrs. Steadman unwisely suggested that the couple would look ridiculous walking down the aisle when Nancye was nearly six feet tall and Gordon a mere five foot six. The unhappy result was that Nancye never married and Gordon chose for his wife his father's nurse and ended his days in bedroom slippers living in the kitchen.

Now we come to the Bouchers. Audrey, the younger daughter, was in my form at the High School but we never cared much for each other. She was very staid and had little sense of humour, whereas her elder sister, Joyce, was a ball of fire. I met her first at her engagement party to Cyril Uwins, then an object of much interest because he was recovering from a broken neck caused by a plane crash. Later he became highly revered as Chief Test Pilot for Bristol Aeroplane Company. Never shall I forget the day when we watched his tiny red plane soar up and up until it disappeared into the blue leaving only the roar of the engine as he achieved a new height record.

Another family were the Badocks. Sir Stanley was a leading light in Bristol University and Lady Badock's mother had founded Badminton School, with which I have always been more or less in contact. The school had many foreign students from the first and some of us joined the Badock's English Speaking Union. The Badock family too were fond of party-giving, they lived in grounds which contained Henleaze Lake, where we often fished and swam, and many were the dances at Holmewood.

I remember the days when the University Tower was being built, an object of great interest to John and me. One day we found the entrance unbarred and on an impulse climbed up the winding staircase until we reached the top where the great bell was lashed securely to a bar. With the usual foolishness of youth we managed to untie this rope and without warning the huge bell began to swing from side to side causing ear-splitting reverberations. Terrified we rushed down. I can't imagine why nobody was there to stop us, but we reached the ground unobserved and walked rapidly back towards Clifton.

Another interesting family were the Horace Walkers. I wonder how many Bristolians now know that Wanscow Walk was derived from the names of the three men who owned that property, Wansbrough, Cowlin and Walker. Horace became Sheriff of Bristol more than once. He and his wife had two daughters and they entertained lavishly in their Stoke Bishop home. Phyllis, the elder daughter, and I went frequently to Oxford for balls and the Varsity matches, and there she fell in love with a delightfully modest man, a fine cricketer and as English-looking as possible.

Came the wedding, a huge affair. Of course the bridegroom's family appeared in the church, one after the other they walked in, each darker than the last. They were Indian. Imagine the gasps of horror and amazement from the congregation! According to my parents, Horace never mentioned the matter and I suppose all might have gone well had Alec continued to practise in his London firm of solicitors, but his father was taken ill so Alec decided to return to India where an enormous connection awaited him. There was trouble at once, for while Phyllis enjoyed all the privileges of the ruling whites, Alec was forbidden entry to any hotel or club. Before long they were quarrelling publicly and the marriage eventually ended in divorce.

Act 2, Scene 2: My Career Takes Off

On the work front, there were endless recitals for charity, sometimes at the home of a brilliant violinist, Doris Vevers, sometimes with Beryl Titchman and Norman Jones, two magnificent pianists, sometimes with Hedley Goodall, sometimes with Edgar Harrison. I always believed in wearing attractive clothes. I remember particularly a midnight blue satin confection, absolutely simple, but beautifully cut, and a dramatic outfit which was trimmed with black fur, which was actually created for me when I played in *Sacred Flame* for Hedley.

I owe a huge debt of gratitude to Hedley. He gave me the most wonderful opportunities for playing in every type of production, from comedy to tragedy. I remember one or two particular incidents. For instance, we were playing in *Canaries Sometimes Sing*, a Frederick Lonsdale comedy, which we took to Wales. I had to open the play and I mastered two bars of the *Moonlight Sonata* which I played with great aplomb – playing was not my forté and really the only bars which were sufficiently dramatic were the two opening ones. On this particular night I played the two bars, then I played them again because I couldn't play any more, and then again and again. At that point my partner had still not come on, so I had to feign some sort of exit and go in search of him. But whereas Percy, the canary, behaved impeccably throughout, my leading man – Leslie Everett – was missing and the stage manager finally collared him in the local bar. We had to start the play all over again.

In 1932, Hedley produced *Hassan* – a delightful costume was designed for me with a bare midriff but that of course was not allowed. Barbara Macrae and I played in many of Hedley's productions and even when she and I were running rival schools we never had a cross word but enjoyed each other's work, unlike some of our students, who became very partisan. I always thought that Barbara's verse speaking was exquisitely creative and better than ours, but we, the Hartly Hodders – Hartly 'Horrors' was our nickname at that time – were very much more adventurous in our drama training and productions. As far as Clifton was concerned my first Tiny Tots production in Clifton Parish Church was with the sisters Patricia and

Katherine Roberts and their friend Diana Finch. They were all 5 to 6 years old, so I had special furniture built for them in pale green. Patricia later proved to be a wonderful pianist and one of the most versatile pupils I have ever had. She worked and played for me right up until World War II. A real trouper. I was sad when she married and went on to other things and sadder still to learn of her recent death.

By this time I had collected a number of enthusiastic and gifted students, among them Joyce Grylls, whose daughter Honor later also became one.

Nineteen thirty three, the year when the decree nisi was made absolute, I reckon to have been the high point of my career, when thanks to the training I had in Paris several years previously and to the perceptive encouragement of Douglas, I directed three beautiful mime plays, then considered to be most innovative. We played them in Bristol Zoological Gardens and then in gardens all round Somerset and we reckoned that some eight or nine thousand people must have supported us. The first mime was *The Birthday of the Infanta*, based on the beautiful short story by Oscar Wilde. I was lucky to have a fine actor, Bobby Dixon, as the dwarf. We created a horrific make-up for him, while the huge cast wore wonderful Elizabethan-style costumes. The second and third were my original stories, so hadn't quite the magic of *The Infanta*. They were entitled respectively, *The Enchanted Garden* and *The Pipes of Pan*, both lending themselves to splendidly imaginative costumes and treatment.

All this time in the early thirties I had been doing small productions at Weirfield School in Taunton and the first important one which we did in the Town Hall was called *Lady Precious Stream* and this was quite delightful because it was stylised. I only knew that I had to do it this way because I had seen the London production of this same play, but of course hardly anybody in Taunton had seen anything of the kind, so it created a great sensation. Soon after this we, the Hartly Hodder Players, went in for the British Drama League Festival. We presented *The Distant Drum* by Ivor Brown and we won triumphantly in Taunton and Bristol but were knocked out at Stratford in the third round. The most important production I ever did at Weirfield was Shaw's *St. Joan*. I must be one of the few people to whom Shaw gave permission to present an abridged version of the play; I felt that those huge long speeches were impossible material for young schoolgirls to cope with.

It was an incredible success. My girl who played Joan, Doreen Woodward, would have made a wonderful actress and I always hoped that she would go on to RADA and make it her profession, but like so many people she was waylaid by some attractive man and went off to other spheres. On the other hand, there was another little girl called Frances Cohen who played Stogumber. I have seen this play probably twelve or fourteen times but strangely enough never have I been so moved as I was by Frances Cohen's interpretation of Stogumber when he returns to the stage having seen Joan burned. Actually we had repercussions from that performance because both Frances and Doreen were so involved and so moved by their roles that they had what would now be called nervous breakdowns and that taught me never to try to enlarge too far the consciousness of young people. I am sure it is a dangerous thing to do. Doreen was the first of our students to get an LRAM which in those days was the height of achievement and something we had been working towards for a number of years.

For some time I had been looking to find something really arresting and yet at the same time suitable for schoolgirls. It was very difficult as you have to remember that I was dealing with an all-girls' school and not every play is fit to be played by the same sex. Of course I had done all the main Shakespeare ones that I thought were possible and I wanted to get away from that when it suddenly struck me what a wonderful story Christ's Crucifixion is. So I looked through St. John and found how exciting it was. I had it typed out and put in a number of interjections and shouts of 'murder him', 'crucify him' etc., etc., but when we started to rehearse there was very little reaction from the children. So I had the bright idea – at least what I thought was a bright idea – of suggesting that the children went through the Bible with a fine toothcomb to find anything in biblical language which was indicative of anger or contempt that could be incorporated in the conversation which was being shouted by the villagers as they accompanied Christ up the hill.

One day I thought they weren't making nearly enough noise and I got up and said, "Look, look you hate this man, now come along, try and think of somebody you hate, try and think of anything that annoys you, make it your feeling, concentrate on it, do something with it, now – let's do this over again." Of course in those days we couldn't let anybody show as Christ but we chose a very nice girl and she had a great cross on her back and over the top of the wall you could see this cross, occasionally held fairly high and more frequently lost behind the wall, as He stumbled. We started again. I said, "Now maximum noise, now really hate this man, now get on with it, get on with it" and we were getting on with it, we were really getting something out of it, it was simply terrific, when the door was flung open and my headmistress came through. "Miss Hodder," she said, "what *are* you doing?"

45

There was absolute silence. I mean in those days we all knew how to behave ourselves and when the headmistress entered, whatever we were doing we stopped immediately. I said to her, "They're rehearsing," so she said "Well, I realise they're rehearsing but what are they rehearsing?" So without thinking I said "The Crucifixion". Well, I thought she was going to have a fit, her face went scarlet, she said "The Crucifixion" in a sort of strangled voice. "Stop it," she said, "it's sacrilegious" – and we were not allowed to do it. So there we were within about three weeks or so of our production and I had to start and think of something entirely different. Actually it was *Boy With A Cart* which was quite a pleasant thing to do but nothing like as exciting I can assure you as my interpretation of The Crucifixion.

For my own entertainment, the Colston Hall always provided magnificent concerts, that's where I met Kreisler and Solomon, the latter still to my mind the finest interpreter of Chopin I ever heard. Have I mentioned the Hippodrome? I remember that opening show, *The Sands of Dee*, where the hero on a horse swam across the water to rescue the girl tied to a stake downstage. Well of course for the first two or three days the surge of water swept over the orchestra and the first row of the stalls. By the time we saw the show they had erected a large glass screen which shielded us from the worst of the watery impact.

Professionally I had to deal with my aunt, Lallie Hicks. She was a great influence on my early life but we gradually grew apart. To begin with she disapproved of divorce in general and of mine in particular. Also I found her difficult to deal with in professional matters. She had for so long occupied a unique position among teachers and examiners for our subject, Speech and Drama, that perhaps she felt a little jealous of my success.

By this time, 1935, she had taken Phyllis Smale into partnership. Phyllis was a brilliant actress who later created the radio character of Mrs. Luscombe. Lallie was always hoping that Phyllis would marry but we all knew that the men who made up Lallie's world were in love with her and not with Phyllis. Later on Phyllis married happily and they had a delightful daughter, Harriet.

About this time Hedley's production of *Hamlet* was a watershed in the standard of Bristol's amateur theatre. We played in the Victoria Rooms on a set which had steep steps leading up and steep steps leading down, and across the back of the stage a couple of planks. It looked stunning with its drapes and was a splendid entry for the 'royals'. I was playing Gertrude in a beautiful cream and gold medieval gown and a high medieval steeple head-dress, quite difficult to wear even on *terra firma*, but when, as a vertigo sufferer, I had to cross that narrow strip of timber and then descend the stairs to the throne room level I can't tell you what I endured; however, it had to be done and my producer told me to do it and I did, but I shudder to this day at the memory.

The Bristol Shakespeare Society then decided that they must do better, so they chose the 'Scottish play' and asked me to direct it. I had produced several cut versions of Shakespearean comedies at Weirfield – with a schoolgirl cast, of course – so this was a real challenge, which needless to say I accepted. Our venue was the YMCA, a detestable auditorium with a stage several feet too high above the ground. My Macbeth was a Scotsman, so he had the right accent and he was quite a good actor, but he had never played Shakespeare before and he found blank verse difficult to memorise. Phyllis Macklin played Lady Macbeth, looking absolutely beautiful, I have a wonderful photograph of her in her sleepwalking scene, while Macduff was played by a student of mine, Bill Flint, who later married one of my Weirfield pupils and who, after a gallant career in World War II, became an examiner for the Guildhall. I have never heard that scene where Macduff learns of the callous murder of his wife and children more poignantly played than by Bill in this production.

A month or so earlier I had been up to London and saw for the first time actors making an entrance through the auditorium. I was very impressed with this innovation and decided that this was just what was needed for the arrival of the invading army through Dunsinane Forest. I impressed on my company the need for silence regarding this. As costs were high we had only one combined dress rehearsal plus lighting in the theatre and by midnight we had only just reached Act 5. The actors were exhausted and I still had to complete my lighting plot, so I simply showed them how they had to scramble up from ground level to stage level, and sent them home.

Unfortunately, when it came to the actual performance, the cast bursting through the rear door with blackened faces and carrying branches so frightened the audience in the back rows that they reacted loudly and by the time the actors reached the rostra which had been placed there to help them scale the heights, the weight of the branches and pikes made it almost impossible for them to reach stage level. A couple of them had to be killed and unfortunately they fell on the feet of those sitting in the front row – they made a fuss, too. Can you imagine the tumult? If I had had any sense I should have lowered the curtain, but these were circumstances I had never encountered before so I just let matters take their course.

In the meantime Macduff had entered, expecting to find Macbeth on stage, but Macbeth had missed his cue in the general riot, so each had to search for the other, thus ruining the terrific climax of the encounter and fight. By this time the audience were hysterical with laughter and at last I had the presence of mind to lower the front tabs. Everyone says *Macbeth* is the most unlucky play and certainly this was the most disastrous experience of my theatrical life.

There was a later incident when I was judging the play in Scotland – in those days we had to give an immediate public assessment and result. Well, I'd hated the Lady Macbeth, she'd played the part like some Glasgow innkeeper's wife, so I felt I must tackle the best bits, and some of the performances were very good indeed, and I was rather hesitant to begin with, so I said "Well, now I will deal with Lady Macbeth. As you all know this is considered the most difficult of any Shakespearean role. . ." Whereupon the actress, who was sitting just in front of me in the first row of the stalls, flung back her head and interrupted very loudly, "Well, Miss Hartly Hodder, it was nae trouble to me!"

One day Douglas telephoned to say that he had met an old Oxford friend who had just been invalided out of India and was at a loose end, so he had invited him to dinner that night. That was fine because we had already asked another old Oxford friend, David, who was the new Bishop of Llandaff. David and I were having a drink together when I heard the front door open and went out into the hall and saw the saddest, most emaciated face I have ever encountered. I stopped short and said, "Oh, what can ail thee Knight at Arms, alone and palely loitering?" whereupon he replied at once, "I met a Lady in the Meads full beautiful, a fairy's child," and I knew that he had fallen in love with me. His name was Gareth Vaughan-Jones.

We had a strange evening discussing the rights and wrongs of tolerance versus intolerance. I was having one of my tolerant periods; David, of course, was strictly Church of Wales, Douglas was the most tolerant man I've ever met, and Gareth had violent views on everything. We talked far into the night and when they departed, David said "It's been wonderful to meet you Eileen, but if I had the power I'd burn you at the stake; you are the most dangerous woman I have ever met!"

In the morning Gareth telephoned and said "Are you going to marry Douglas?" to which I replied "I honestly don't know, although we've discussed the matter frequently." "Well, tell him not to bother, I'm going to marry you." I laughed and pointed out that he had no job, no prospects,

Top Grandmother Hodder, with baby Clement and, standing, Lallie. *Right* Mother, aged 12. *Below* Wedding of Edith Kate Barron (mother) and Clement Hartly Hodder (father).

I

Edith Kate, Eileen's mother.

Eileen revisiting Middleton House.

Eileen and Jacko the pony with head gardener at Middleton House.

The young horsewoman on Charlie.

IV

Eileen hugging father, with John and Fitz.

Two addresses in Apsley Road: No.5 and No.19.

John driving Eileen's Lagonda, 1936.

Clifton High School, 1918: Eileen is on far right in middle row, aged 15.

The school some years before Eileen's time there.

Eileen at the Lord Mayor's garden party
at The Chantry, Abbots Leigh, with Mrs
Clifford Steadman and Miss Nancye
Steadman, 1932.

VIII

and that I had very sybaritic tastes. But from that day onwards, every Saturday for three years, he proposed to me and always brought me red roses – if he had had a good week, it was a great bouquet; if it was a poor one, a single bloom.

Gareth was a six-footer, broad-shouldered and a good sportsman; he played both rugby and cricket for his college, but never achieved a Blue. He adored Latin which he spoke and wrote as easily as he did English. He used to read very slowly moving his head from side to side and having once read, he never forgot, whereas I skim down the middle of each page, remember for a moment, but the next day have forgotten. When he was born his nose was slightly injured so from one side view he was ugly and from the other he was handsome, a physical dichotomy which was reflected in his personality. It was like being married to a schizophrenic – perhaps that's what he was!

He and his brother Idris and sister Gwenith were brought up very strictly in the Forest of Dean where the Sabbath was a day of dread, constant church services, endless questions on the sermons and collects during lunch, no toys or games in the afternoon and then more church in the evening. No wonder they both rebelled against religion. They were lucky enough to be sent to Bristol Grammar School, then under the inspired leadership of Ted Barton and his beautiful wife Bertie, a diminutive form of Bertha. Ted was a man of many parts, a brilliant classical scholar, with a profound knowledge of architecture, travel, literature, philosophy and painting; he was also a good dancer. He could lecture on all of these with equal ease and humour. As it happens, he was also instrumental in inspiring Douglas, another Bristol Grammar School boy, in his love of literature and fine books. The two Vaughan-Jones boys were obviously university material and Idris gained a scholarship to Merton, where he afterwards remained as Senior Tutor, while Gareth went to New College.

During those years of party going, Gareth and I were always on the verge of meeting but always missed each other. His farewell to Oxford was typical of the man. He went for his viva, which was chaired by that brilliant man and good friend to us, the Emeritus Professor of Latin, H. W. Garrod. He addressed Gareth and said "Tell me Vaughan-Jones Minor, you don't seem to have answered any questions on your set books, Plato and Aristotle," to which Gareth replied, "Emeritus Professor, it is a habit of mine never to answer questions on books I haven't read." Of course, he ought to have been sent down but the authorities in their wisdom awarded him a BA Second Class Honours. Another of his tutors summed up the situation when he bade him farewell with these sadly prophetic words: "Goodbye Vaughan-Jones, you have a brilliant future behind you."

When Gareth left Oxford he went to India working for the Oxford University Press throughout that sub-continent. Almost as soon as he arrived there, he shared a house with five other young men. One day he was browsing through the *Radio Times* when he saw a photograph of me and at once vowed that he would marry that girl! He loved India, particularly Ceylon, where he found the women brilliant and beautiful. Unfortunately, for all his charm and great intelligence, he had a fatal weakness – he drank too much, and the splendid existence during those last decades of the Raj, from the regal balls at Government House to the bands of Indian servants in his own home, proved his undoing. He contracted the deadliest form of malaria and was invalided out. As he owed money everywhere his unfortunate father had to pay his debts and bring him home.

Unhappy and ill he was advised by his doctors to live a quiet country life for a couple of years: one side of him loved this, he rented a tiny cottage in the middle of Wales, his only companion an adored cat, and there he wrote his first and only novel which was published by Constable. It was a satirical novel but the title has gone to the grave with him and in spite of searching with his friends and relations in the Bodleian and the British Library I have never been able to locate the book – we don't even know under what name it was published. He and his publisher were sued because apparently everyone mentioned in its pages was identifiable. The judge awarded the plaintiffs the then huge sum of £2,000 and Gareth returned neither sober nor wiser to his mountain hideaway. Small wonder that I greeted him with Keats's words when at last he ventured back into Bristol to seek comfort from his old university friend Douglas. He had a wonderful way with all animals – had he been born later he would have found his niche in a wildlife programme on the BBC – but with his active brain he became bored with this solitary existence and began again to drink too much.

In spite of darkening political shadows and our financial difficulties, Douglas and I were blissfully happy, we complemented each other. He was a very interesting character, generous, intelligent, with a tremendous sense of humour, a classical education which meant that he made love most excitingly and above all he was keenly interested in all things around him. His only fault was his extreme untidiness. He would remove his tie in the drawing room, throw first one shoe and then the other into the hall, leave his trousers in the bathroom, and what was left littered our bedroom. We had frequent battles over this. And he left the top of the toothpaste open. But we could argue about the relative values of plays and films and novels and poems.

He introduced me to Evelyn Waugh and John Betjeman, he knew them at Oxford, and he greatly enlarged my musical knowledge. I already knew and played the classics, Beethoven, Bach, Mozart, Schubert, but Delius, Debussy, Dvorak and Walton were new to me. As I needed a wide musical background for the mimes he was an invaluable help; also he believed in me and in my creative abilities. I had started to train as an examiner for the Guildhall School of Music and Drama when I was about twenty three but now, thanks to the generous guidance of people like Guy Pertwee, Daniel Roberts, Florence Moore and Dorothy Dayus, I was invited to join the board as one of their youngest members and from then onwards I travelled throughout the United Kingdom and both parts of Ireland where I had many delights and adventures.

The 1930s, with the Depression, were difficult years for fine book publishing and selling, and Douglas experienced his share of ups and down, not helped by the bankruptcy of an American agent and a defaulting Australian bookseller. Ever resilient, he had bought an old printing machine and set up his celebrated Clover Hill Press, although this was not to come into its own until some years after Hitler's war. He knew all the great creators of modern typefaces and lettering, the two most important being Stanley Morison and Eric Gill, and early in his career had published *Art and Love*, a collection of Gill's engravings. Gill and Morison were frequent visitors to us and occasionally we went to the strange Bohemian establishment Gill set up, first of all at Capel-y-ffin in the Black Mountains in Wales and later at Pigotts, a farmhouse near High Wycombe. Eric lived and worked with his family in most primitive conditions, which Douglas enjoyed but I longed for hot baths and a comfortable bed. There Eric designed the lion for me which I later adopted as a crest for the school with a motto suggested by Douglas, 'Plaudite Omnes'. For non-Latin readers may I say that means 'Let the Audience Applaud'. All my notepaper, flyers – although we didn't call them flyers in those days, only notices – Christmas cards, invitations, programmes were printed in green and very attractive they look in my scrapbook some sixty years later.

Douglas and I were both workaholics. Many a time we would dress for the evening and leave about 4 o'clock in our open AC car and travel that tortuous road to London, stopping in Savernake for a sandwich and a drink. I am always fascinated by forests, they are so mysterious, and I know both Savernake and the Forest of Dean in every sort of weather and at all times of the night and day. We would arrive in London just in time for the 8.30 curtain up and of course we had to travel all the way back again. This time we'd share eggs and bacon at a wayside café with splendid lorry drivers and reach home about four in the morning, but ready to restart work at nine o'clock.

We saw all the great stars, Gertrude Lawrence, Noel Coward, the Lunts, Edith Evans as a delicious Mrs. Sullen in Farquhar's *Beau Stratagem*, we went to Covent Garden, we saw the fabulous Diaghilev Ballet – never shall I forget the excitement of our first *Petroushka* – and back in Bristol there were plenty of good productions, not least at the dear old Princes Theatre where Matheson Lang and Marie Tempest were among many great artists who toured.

I shall certainly never forget those special favourites, the Rapier Players at the Little Theatre, a company run by Ronald Russell and his wife, Peggy Ann Wood, where later a dozen or more of my students learned their theatre craft as assistant stage managers.

When I look back at those days I marvel at our energy. I was working from September 1st to July 31st, often sixteen hours a day, and yet not only did I have this social life but I also became very involved in local politics, largely because my mother had her first heart attack. In the early 1930s I flirted briefly with the Communists but then decided to become a paid-up member of the Conservative Party instead.

One of the highlights of the Clifton Season was the Lifeboat Ball. My mother had formed a strong Ladies' Committee with Mary, Lady Cadbury, the first chairman, my mother the first secretary, and Elsie Clifford, the treasurer. Mother always gathered together like-minded friends, hard-working, dedicated, and interestingly enough this has persisted right up to the present day where I find that the young women are always ready to give of their best. I must mention Liz Harvey, who year after year used to put her house at our disposal so that we could build up a reputable sale of beautiful and often unusual articles.

After a time this function became so huge that we moved to Ashton Court in order to accommodate the ever widening range of goods. I joined the Ladies' Committee as a very young woman and served on it for 62 years, during three of which I was chairman. Various things happened during that time. I was invited as chairman to attend the Royal Garden Party at Buckingham Palace, then later there came the Investiture where my mother was created a Life Member of the Institution. Next in 1993 I was awarded the Life Boat Gold Medal at a ceremony hosted by the Duke of Kent, to which I was allowed to bring a party of some twenty people, which included my two nieces and their husbands.

(The last Ball I attended was at Chew Court, the home of Mr. and Mrs. Peter Ferguson, when the tickets were £50 each, a far cry from £2 for a double charged at the first dance in Clifton. This whole affair had become extremely sophisticated, a champagne reception followed by a gourmet meal.)

Interval: World War II

And so we come to September 1939. The three years before were dreadfully sad, several of my best friends went to the Spanish Civil War and three were killed, and Hitler's threat became ever more sinister. I had started this era as a pacifist but as evidence of Nazi cruelty became ever clearer I gradually came to believe that England should oppose him. It's very hard to exchange one set of strongly held values and beliefs and to accept others. Gareth believed at once that we should fight. Douglas, who had converted me to pacifism, was deeply disturbed by events but felt inclined to wait and see. My father believed that Hitler would be the saviour of the German nation, so one was pulled hither and thither. My young friends loathed Mussolini and Hitler; my older ones, who had sad and vivid memories of 1914, couldn't bring themselves to face another appalling situation. My teaching saved me then, as it has several times since. Many young people depended on me for understanding and support so I was forced to continue to work, to read, to study.

Gareth became bitterly jealous of Douglas. We had begun as a relationship 'à trois' but by this time I had fallen in love with Gareth as well, so I now know, as I did then, that it is possible to love two men simultaneously.

My brother John joined the RNVR, Gareth, romantic as ever, insisted on joining the local Artillery Regiment as an ordinary gunner – this annoyed me very much indeed because he looked so awful in his ill-fitting uniform, the material was so cheap. He had an idea that the Army had been made democratic and that this is what he should do, but by the time hostilities really began, the first time we went into an hotel where we were both well known, we were greeted by the signs 'Officers Only' and 'Other Ranks' and had to find our way through the meaner door.

It also annoyed me that Douglas, who had just got a permanent job at the BBC and who had suffered so desperately before with that painful struggle to make a success of his bookshop, refused to join up – I think he didn't want to face the fact that war was inevitable now.

So this was really the moment when the break came between Douglas and me. I thought the hard facts made it inevitable that we had to fight Hitler.

The Saturday after Chamberlain had returned from Berlin, I was alone in the flat and on impulse I telephoned Cornwall where Gareth was stationed and said to him, "Gareth, I'll marry you!" Of course he nearly dropped the telephone because he'd been trying to do this for the last five years. So we got married. He had to get a special licence, and because I was divorced, no correct clergyman in Bristol would marry us, but dear old William Rogers, one of the few really Christian clergymen I've ever known, who had a funny little church, St. Aiden's, consented to marry us. We rushed over there and were married at 8 o'clock in the morning, with none of our family or friends present.

Afterwards I went back to the flat alone, and Gareth went back to Cornwall. I cheered myself up by going to have my hair done. And there, in the glossy magazine I picked up, it said that Scorpios and Capricorns shouldn't marry as we shared each other's bad points! It was not a very happy day.

Somehow we got through the week, and at the end of it war was declared. I went down, I think it was to the Council House, to enrol as an ambulance driver. When I got there all the forms had been taken and somebody said to me out of the blue, "Can you drive?" I said I could, to which he replied, "Come along then, I'll take you with one of the big vans to see how you handle it."

So off I went with the most charming chap, who was an inspector with what was then the old Bristol Tramways Company. He was very complimentary about my driving. Without having signed any forms I was swept into a furniture van and we went over to a church hall on Bedminster Down where we were told to bed down for the night: there were dozens of us, bare boards, cold water, nothing else, not a toothbrush between us.

No sooner had we bedded down than my leader said I ought to get to know the district, so I drove the furniture van through Bedminster with no lights and not the vaguest idea where I was going. We got back at 3 a.m. and I had to find my place on the bare boards where I tried to sleep until morning. At that point I asked if I could telephone home because no-one knew where I was, but they wouldn't allow me because security must be kept very tight.

That went on for a couple of days and I drove around Bristol in the dark; I was exhausted so at least I slept on my bare wooden patch, and on the Sunday at about seven we heard that fatal sound wailing through the silence, that sound of terror we were to know so well: the first air raid alert. World War II had really begun.

By this time John had been given his last leave from his MTB and when he got back he found my family anxious about me. Somehow he managed to find out where I was stationed and out he came to Bedminster and, ignoring the complaints of my superior, he took me back home to No.5 Apsley Road where we were all reunited as a family. We then had to decide what we were going to do.

It was clear that evacuees would be sent from London to Bristol and that as we had a large house and not many people, it would be commandeered for evacuees. It was obviously more sensible to get in touch with people we knew and offer them refuge, which we did, and the Guildhall sent me students and somebody else called from Devon and soon we had a house entirely full of youngsters, and very charming most of them were, too. By this time Gareth had been moved to Compton Greenfield, near Almondsbury, so I could get out to see him.

I was soon overwhelmed with work. The previous year, the two schools where I taught, in Burnham-on-Sea and Taunton, had realised war was coming and knowing that younger members of staff would be called up, had each asked me whether I would take over the teaching of English, as well as Speech and Drama, which I was pleased to do. It was lucky that I did, for Burnham had no rail connection, so I was allowed a permit and extra coupons for petrol, since English, unlike Drama, was considered an important Foundation subject. So I was in great demand for lifts, and provided I stuck to my correct routes and if I free-wheeled down every incline, however slight, I could just manage on the petrol allowance. I had to drive from Bristol to Taunton, Taunton to Burnham and Burnham back to Bristol. For £95 I bought a little Ford 8 and did 92,000 miles in her; at the end of the war I sold the car for £700 (the solitary bargain of my life)!

The first year wasn't so bad except that the weather was terrible. Gareth, who was now stationed on a farm near Avonmouth, succumbed to an attack of dengue fever, and by this time he was heartily sick of being a gunner. There were only one or two light-hearted moments and one of them concerned geese. Gareth had a wonderful way with animals and birds, and he adored strange things like geese. I was always frightened of them, but whenever he appeared, they came flapping towards him, making the most frightful noise, and the Sergeant-Major used to rush up and say, "Vaughan-Jones, call off them asterisk geese," and Gareth had to lead them back to their pen, because they would always follow him.

By this time, the bombing had started and the noise and the mess that the guns made were worse than any bomb. The roads were inches deep in bits of shrapnel. One day I was out at the camp seeing Gareth when the siren went, and of course I couldn't leave. I just stayed there quivering by the side of the road. I could hear this plane coming over and the guns opened up, a most terrible noise and I thought I was going to be killed or deafened for ever. Then there was a really shattering noise and one of Gareth's platoon came rushing up to me saying, "Oh, Mrs. VJ, Mrs. VJ, we got 'im, we got 'im, swastikickle and all." I think it was the only time they ever hit anything.

We had month after month of snow in that first year and of course there was no-one to clear it, so the snow gradually built up right across the roads to the top of the hedges. When I drove down to Taunton, the whole road was just like the surface of the moon, with me in my little car bumping along on top. There were no car heaters then, so I used to go with a rug wrapped round me and one hot water bottle on my feet and another on my tummy and they just about lasted the journey.

I hardly ever travelled the road alone; I picked everyone up, man, woman and child because one did in those days, you never thought of not offering a lift. I never had anything but courteous thanks and often very delightful conversations. One bitterly cold day I picked up an old gipsy, a fearful smell filled the car but I had to endure it until we reached Bridgwater. She thanked me profusely and handed me an enormous roll of filthy paper. That evening when I unwrapped the package, I found it contained dozens of clothing coupons, enough to dress me and all my friends and students for the rest of the war. But all through the war I was terrified, not of driving on my own, I was used to that, but of the bombs, and as I have very sensitive hearing, I can't tell you how I suffered. I hate remembering it really.

By this time Gareth had pulled a few strings and had got out of the ranks and into the Education Corps where he was much happier, because he was doing a really good job there. In the second year of the war he was stationed in Cornwall, and that was a fascinating time because he had charming people round him to fraternise with – Leonard Sachs, Michael Soames, Robert Holmes. At Christmas, Gareth decided to put on a pantomime, *Dick Whittington*. He wrote the script in rhyming couplets, Leonard produced it, Soames danced the Cat and Robert played the Dame. You had to seize on everything you could to make it fun, otherwise life was so bleak and horrible.

At one time I was ill with severe sinusitis and joined Gareth in Suffolk for a fortnight's leave. We were given the head gamekeeper's cottage in the middle of a great wood. It was enchanting, roses and honeysuckle-covered, with a magnificent view cut through the trees. If you sat on the 'loo' the squirrels and foxes would often look through the tiny window. There was a delightful black kitten there who, one night, to show how greatly he loved me, climbed up the fencing, leapt through the open window and deposited a nearly dead baby rabbit on my chest. Chaos ensued as Gareth found a candle and matches to light it. Country sounds all around, owls at night, larks all day, fought a battle against the hideous continuous roar and throb of the planes.

The days flew by and I returned to Bristol but was still so ill that my doctors advised an operation. So on the day of the first daylight raid on Bristol I was in the Homeopathic Hospital, I heard the alarm as I was wheeled in to the operating theatre at 9 o'clock and the 'all clear' as I recovered consciousness at 6 o'clock. I had taken all this quite calmly, I'd been feeling ill for so long and had been in such pain that I used to lay my head on my hands and pray that my next student would either be late or absent. They never were!

My Taunton classes were devastated when I told them I had to leave them in the care of one of my staff for a fortnight. For the first week I had dozens of well wishing cards from them, the second week I had nothing. But I didn't expect any more attention. However, I didn't make as speedy a recovery as I had hoped and my doctors insisted that I took a third week off. The member of staff who had taken over from me had greatly enjoyed her fortnight and spoke enthusiastically about the work she'd had from them. However that third week they were unbelievably rebellious and difficult to handle and when I returned at the beginning of the fourth week, they continued this hostile attitude and we didn't get on really happy terms again until after half term. Wasn't it strange? I'm sure that the young find illness very difficult to understand. Now I'm old and quite ill again I've discovered it is not only the young who don't understand how you feel.

I think everyone ought to have an illness at about the age of twenty, not anything too serious, but just enough to experience the extraordinary inability to lift a hand off the sheet. Anyhow, as soon as I was well enough, I restarted my West Country trek and a student who lived in Bridgwater suggested that I break my journey there and have tea and a rest before continuing to Taunton. This seemed an excellent idea so I stopped and rang the bell and a very old lady came to let me in. I wasn't surprised that she was old but I was horrified to see an open wound down one side of her face, I must admit that I found it an horrendous experience to eat tea opposite her. What really shook me was that on departure, my student remarked on my good luck in making such a satisfactory recovery because her mother had undergone a similar operation, as I must have observed. I would never have faced the operation had I realised that danger. This was indeed one of the occasions when ignorance was bliss.

I've already remarked on the isolation of Taunton from Bristol; during the war this was even more pronounced, luckily for a number of people, as it turned out. It a very emotional period, especially for the young, as was later the arrival of the American troops with their money and super-abundance of goodies which exacerbated the problem. Before I knew where I was one of my Taunton students announced that she was pregnant and could I help her, so I did the only possible thing and took her into my flat in Bristol and cared for her until the baby was born. She was the only student who had the courage to return to her home with an illegitimate child.

It must be very difficult for those born in these easy-going days to understand the horror – not too strong a word – felt by parents and friends when this problem arose. In fact, I succoured three pregnant Somerset students here in Bristol and four from Bristol with friends of mine in Taunton. One, such an adorably pretty girl, asked my advice when she later fell in love – should she tell her fiancé? I hesitated for some time and finally advised against it. She had a wonderful wedding, even in wartime everyone turned out in top hats and finery. It was the June when *My Love* won the Derby so of course there was a constant buzz of conversation among the guests as someone with a radio related the progress and final triumph of the horse. I wish I could tell you that all this had a happy ending but alas! at their first row, the husband called his bride a 'whore' and before long there was a divorce.

The other girls took my advice and fostered their babies and I hope conveniently forgot the whole episode. Many years later I encountered one of these young women at a cocktail party; I started to acknowledge her but she cut me dead. This upset me temporarily until Gareth laughed and said "Why worry, you remind her of something which she would rather forget" – and then of course I understood and when we met on other occasions I just waved and moved away.

Some time during 1940 a single plane dropped a set of four bombs near Apsley Road: the first fell on the Downs, harmlessly by the funnel at the top of Pembroke Road, the second fell through the roof of No.5. Fortunately it didn't explode but lodged in the strengthened floor of the billiard room, so we spent the rest of the war with a tarpaulin over the roof. It was very chilly! The third fell on the house at the top of St. John's Road, completely destroying it, but fortunately Dr. Hall and his wife had gone into their air raid shelter. These were dreadful nights and days of hellish noise, many of my friends were so brave they hardly stopped talking as the bomb whined its way down and the roar of the explosion followed. Being such a coward I always expected the worst and was never surprised to find that Shakespeare had as always said it all: 'Cowards die many times before their death'.

I loathed the noise of guns and bombs, I hated the war, hated the blackness. I always expected the worst, but I seized upon every opportunity to enjoy myself. These were chiefly times when Gareth and I were together, often when he was on leave. We usually found a peaceful spot far removed from the sounds of war, not always, though, for he had by now been sent to the Isle of Wight where he was based in a house with the most beautiful Adam fireplaces which, to his fury, his fellow officers used as dart boards. Anyhow, he got permission to invite me over. On the short crossing we had a submarine scare which was very upsetting, and just after I arrived the Germans attacked the Isle of Wight for the first time and the cinema next to our hotel suffered a direct hit and some one hundred people were killed – they had never had a raid before. While we were there we met John Arlott, poet and local policeman, who afterwards became a great radio personality with his cricket commentaries.

We were fortunate in Bristol that we avoided the doodle-bugs, much more terrifying than the bombs which made a whistling noise as they fell, at least you had some idea where they would land. With the doodle-bug you heard it crash and all you knew was that it hadn't crashed near you so you were safe and with the sort of selfishness that we all seem to experience when in danger, you always said "thank God it didn't hit me". Actually Hitler had built another pad for the launching of the doodle-bugs and they were aimed directly at Bristol; fortunately we were spared that horror.

After a few heavy raids, Clifton friends of ours received a direct hit which destroyed their house. Full of sympathy, I called round and invited them to come and live with me at No. 8. This was a mistake from the beginning because they were three to my one. I decided to give them the dining room and two bedrooms and to share the bathroom and kitchen, while I kept the sitting room and my bedroom. This shouldn't have been too difficult as I was working in Taunton for three days a week, leaving at 9 a.m. and returning about 7 or 8 p.m. I explained that this entailed my using the bathroom first at 8 o'clock. However, next morning when I tried to open the door, it was firmly locked, nor did the husband open it until nearly 8.30! So, for the first time, I was late for my 10 a.m. lesson at Weirfield School.

I returned tired at about 8.30 on the Thursday and went straight to my sitting room to unwind, cope with Guildhall corrections and look at my work for the next day's teaching. The son, a boy of about sixteen, entered without knocking, slouched across the room and turned the wireless on full blast. When I asked him rather sharply to stop, he did so but without speaking, and slammed out of the room. Supper that evening wasn't a very jolly affair but as the siren went pretty soon I didn't make much comment, except to remind them that I always needed the bathroom at 8 o'clock in the morning. I had known them for years but only visited them at party times when the house was immaculate and meals perfectly cooked and served. As we were all going through such traumas I felt that I shouldn't complain too strongly, but when this sort of behaviour continued for three weeks, I could stand it no longer and after an acrimonious flare up, they decided to move out of Bristol and to join one of their relations in Wells. Alas, that was the end of another perfect friendship – strangely enough our paths never crossed again.

Bombs were not the only hazard. There was a Taunton student who developed a passionate lesbian interest in me and it is an incident of which I am extremely ashamed because, knowing the situation as I did, I should always have kept her at arm's length. While we were working in Taunton and I just saw her for lessons this was quite easy. But as the war went on it became more and more difficult to get help of any sort and my flat was always full of pregnant students, and no one to cook for them. So, when this poor lady, braving the bombs and the noise, offered to come up and cook for me, I very unwisely accepted.

Very unwisely and very cruelly accepted because, knowing the situation, I should never have given her such an opportunity to be so near me. As the days went by I became more and more irritated by her, she had a flat stupid red face and rather wispy hair, altogether very unattractive looking. Of course, I was still giving her lessons from time to time. One evening I had had a particularly tiresome day in the studio. I felt completely exhausted when, at around 9 o'clock, there was a timid knock on the door and that hideous red face peered round and said "Eileen, you said you would give me a lesson today." With that I just erupted, screaming, "You know perfectly well I have had a tremendously exhausting day, I cannot give you a lesson, no, no, no, no! I never want to give you another lesson in my life."

On WEDNESDAY, NOVEMBER 30th
at 3 o'clock and 8 o'clock
at
THE WOMEN'S INSTITUTE HALL,
MINEHEAD

EILEEN HARTLY-HODDER
(OF BRISTOL)

will present a programme of
3 one-act plays and an original
sketch by Joyce Hancock.
assisted by her students and

Hedley Goodall
(Producer of the Bristol Drama Club)

in aid of the funds of
The Women's Institute

TICKETS 3/-, 2/- and 1/-

obtainable from all members of the Committee and
Miss Hartly-Hodder. c/o Newcombe's Cafe, Minehead

By this time she had advanced into the studio and I just seized her and hit her, and I hit her and I hit her, and of course she burst into tears, quite naturally, and then I sort of dropped her like a rag doll. The very next morning, not surprisingly, she had packed and she walked out of my studio and out of my life for ever. This is the first time that I have admitted losing my temper and behaving in such a disgraceful manner.

But there are many in Taunton whom I remember with affection and gratitude, all were incredibly kind to me during those often hellish years. Of course German planes often passed over the town so the siren rang out, but they were always on their way to Bristol and never wasted a bomb on us, so I usually slept Wednesday nights, and I mean slept peacefully, which probably explained why I ended the war in reasonably good shape. Certainly from 1940 to 1943 we seldom slept an entire night in Bristol. The Marfell household in Taunton gave me endless hospitality and I used their sitting room for extra lessons and rehearsals after finishing work at Weirfield.

Among the students, there was a delightful young man who was studying to be a professional violinist; unfortunately he fell in love with me and one dreadful Bronte-esque stormy night he arrived for his lesson and then begged to be allowed to spend the night with me. This was of course impossible in any circumstances, but especially in someone else's house and I had to tell him to go, but he remained pleading while poor Mrs. Marfell knocked from time to time as the clock struck first eleven and then eleven thirty. He warned me that he would commit suicide if I turned him away. I'd always been told that people who threaten this never do so, so at last I persuaded this unhappy youth to leave. Alas he hanged himself on a tree just up the road and, as he had a note from me in his pocket, the next day I was involved with the police and certainly needed all the help and affection that the Marfell household could give me.

There was another slight complication at about this time. I had another student, a woman of some forty years, quite rich and very plain, who had a miserable home life because her mother detested her and lavished all her affection on a younger, equally plain sister. This lady had an innate love of poetry, she didn't want to do any examinations but just needed to come to me to read and discuss any kind of good literary work. I felt so sorry for the poor creature, she was so lonely and misunderstood and perhaps unwisely, I consented to take her as a private pupil. She developed a most touching passion for me, but she understood from the beginning what our relationship would have to be.

By this time I had so many private pupils outside the school that I needed more space for rehearsal, preferably with a garden and here several other Taunton families came to my aid, notably the Wards, where mother, father and daughter were all mad on the theatre. Mrs. Marfell was growing very frail so other friends offered me house room and I remember especially Marjorie Spenser Jones, who put up with me and later with Gareth as well until we returned to Clifton. Her kindness and generosity were immense, it can't have been easy for her to put up with such turbulent lodgers.

Of course I was still producing plays in Taunton and some of these productions I took to Bristol. In 1942, *Children in Uniform* with Phyllis Macklin playing the awe-inspiring headmistress, June Monkhouse, Manuela, and Patricia Roberts her friend Lily, won the award at the opening of the Theatre Royal to all amateur clubs in the West Country. The Bristol Savages were so impressed with our performance that they created a beautifully crafted leather box which contained their insignia in the form of a silver necklace, which the adjudicator, the delightful Clifford Bax, hung round my neck and which I still wear on special occasions.

The theatres had closed in 1939 but as people at first thought that it was a phoney war, everything began to open again in 1940. Noel Coward and Laurence Olivier were both at their peak, Coward with *This Happy Breed* in 1942, and his famous play *Brief Encounter* was first seen in 1945; Olivier's film of *Henry V* electrified the nation in 1944. It was just what was needed – it was beautiful, magnificently photographed and with most exciting moments. I remember meeting him some time afterwards when he told me that he had asked one of his company to pass underneath a tree and to hook himself on to a branch and let the horse go on without him; nobody in the company would do it so finally Olivier did it himself and fell down and sprained his ankle!

This was really one of the great periods, if not the greatest period, of English acting, with John Gielgud and Ralph Richardson forming the rest of the quartet of great names. I ought, too, to have mentioned the famous photographer of the time, Angus McBean, because we were lucky enough to persuade him to photograph a couple of our own shows.

As far as Bristol was concerned, Ronnie Russell and Peggy Ann Wood were running the Little Theatre Company on a shoestring for years. Everyone connected with the Little loved them both and enjoyed their rather poverty-stricken productions enormously and Bristol supported them. Then, as the war intensified and the bombing increased, Peggy Ann took the company touring while Ronnie became a warden and rushed about rescuing people from stricken buildings. Strangely enough, they returned to re-open the theatre on Good Friday, April 11th, 1941, immediately after the last great Blitz on the city.

On the fine art front, during the 1930s, I had collected a number of good paintings by David Jones, Paul Nash and Christopher Wood and a local artist John Codner who executed a fine portrait of me. These I loaned to the British Council and they were sent round Britain during the early part of 1939, thanks to the efforts of Eric Walter White who was secretary of the British Council. Then suddenly in 1940 the real war began with nightly, then daily, then occasionally 24-hour raids, so I then decided to sell the paintings, getting only a few hundred pounds for them where now they are worth thousands.

About this time, Douglas's bookshop on the corner of Park Street and Charlotte Street received a direct hit and the whole building went up in flames, destroying the famous sign with its Eric Gill lettering. In fact, that shop was doubly notable in that in the 1920s Roger Fry had painted the hanging sign, with Athena's owl perched on a pile of books, and later Douglas asked Eric to paint the fascia board, and the simple lettering he devised was to spawn the now famous Gill Sans typeface. The destruction of 18 Charlotte Street was a sad loss for intellectual and literary life in Bristol; as well as Douglas' antiquarian bookshop and the studio he shared with Brownie, the building had housed the Clifton Arts Club. We had spent many wonderful evenings there in the thirties.

Various friends from my Douglas period continued to visit me. The artist John Nash asked me to direct him to any houses I knew which had lichen-covered walls and he made many sketches of these. One wintry day he accompanied me on my Taunton journey; on the way back as we climbed Shute Shelve he stopped to look and asked me how many colours I could see in the woods to the left of us, I looked and suggested black, white, several shades of grey and brown, and he took the trouble to point out with his artist's eye the incredible range of hue – about 40.

Another time, J. B. Priestley arrived, working on his celebrated book *English Journey*. As a partner of James and Hodder I could get a pass into Avonmouth docks and Priestley was greatly intrigued with the movements of engines and ships and men. Actually, he disgraced himself. We returned to the flat where I was putting him up and stupidly I put on a stunning black gown for our very meagre meal; as soon as we reached the drawing room he made a pass at me which outraged me, but I could hardly turn him out into the night as he certainly wouldn't have found any shelter.

By 1944, all the forces were rehearsing for the big landing in Europe and Gareth was sent to Winchester and I got special permission to go down and see him for the last few days before embarkation. Winchester was terribly crowded, and we were lucky to get a room. We had to share a single bed, but others were not so lucky – it was the first time I'd ever seen people copulating on flat gravestones, quite an education!

During World War II Gareth established his true worth. Colonel Archie White, Director of the Army Educational Corps, posted him finally to the Guards Armoured Division with instructions to issue a daily news sheet containing comments and contributions, humorous and scurrilous: publications now to be found in the Imperial War Museum among the archives of the Regiment. He had a gallant war record and was twice mentioned in dispatches.

He told me of many incidents in Europe, a few of which I remember, include how he and his clerk, Pizzey, left behind to clear up when the main body was ordered forward, heard the sound of moaning and rescued a poor young woman in labour. He had to cut the umbilical cord with his nail scissors. Alas, owing to the exigencies of war, they were forced to leave them both by the roadside as he and Pizzey had to join the company immediately. When the Guards reached Holland, since no one could speak Dutch and few of the locals knew English, he was able to make contact with various Dutch ministers and officials by talking to them in his favourite classical Latin. These splendid people were only too anxious to supply him with lodgings, food and drink and more fortunately could give him more valuable military information about Panzer movements which were vital to our own commanders.

While in France, they came to a solitary convent and, wanting to know their whereabouts, knocked on the door. After some delay this was opened by the Mother Superior who wept with joy when she recognised English uniforms. She summoned some thirty little Jewish boys from various hiding places and the starving children were instantly fed with chocolate and other rations by the delighted soldiers. When they re-formed and went on their way, Mère Elise said, "Merci, mon Capitaine, Dieu soit bénit. La tendresse est retournée en la France" and she kissed him. We both became great friends with Mère Elise and as I never drank tea I sent her all my tea rations for the rest of the war.

On again across Germany where a terrible stench alarmed everyone, a stench which for some 70 miles grew ever stronger, then around a corner there was Dachau with SS Guards on the perimeter and those dreadful ghosts below. Gareth never forgot the horrors of that concentration camp. The SS men were instantly shot and the Commander and his officers captured even as they were drinking and dancing in their own quarters, which were divided from the camp by a huge wall.

I must mention the relief of Brussels, for the Guards reached that city early one morning. Gareth was on the second tank and within minutes the whole town knew that the British had arrived. There were incredible scenes of rejoicing. Several years later when Gareth and I were at a literary dinner in Bristol, a youngish woman at the end of the table heard that Gareth had been there; she had been a child and had been the one to recognise the black berets as different from the German helmets. When she heard his news she rushed to our seats, dropped on her knees and kissed both his hands as she burst into tears.

After the war, at his advanced age, Gareth was soon discharged and at once started to look for a teaching job armed with the most glowing recommendations from Archie, his CO, David Heneage, a Rabelaisian friend of ours and owner of Fortnum and Mason, and from Lord Carrington and Lord Whitelaw.

During the war my brother John, who knew every nook and cranny of the Normandy and Brittany coasts from our childhood wanderings, was given command of a motor torpedo boat and he and 'Digger' Knight fought a cold and dangerous campaign against German U-Boats and planes. John displayed remarkable courage and among other awards received the DSC and DSO and Bar. My mother and I were delighted to be invited to Buckingham Palace for each investiture. After he received the Bar, John had the honour of being invited to Buckingham Palace for lunch. He told an amusing tale: there was confusion at the table because most of the guests used a knife and fork for the fish course, instead of a fork only, causing consternation to the waiters who had to reset the table. After the final course, the Queen rose to mingle with her guests, at which point the chap opposite John lifted his coffee cup to look at the mark, whereupon the Queen remarked in that icy voice from the far end of the room, "Meissen!" On Monday, 31st May, 1945, John was given the honour of receiving the surrender of the Commander of the German E-Boats.

John had a way of looking at females which always made them fall madly in love with him. He got engaged several times during this history but it was always broken off, so one day we were astonished and infuriated to learn that he had actually married someone in a register office. She was very beautiful and extremely smart – as Patricia was a highly paid model this was to be expected. She obviously thought my brother an excellent catch and was sadly disabused when she found that father was expecting him to return to the Bristol office. Bristol wasn't at all to her taste, nor was the size of John's income!

Their relationship was stormy to say the least, but they were together long enough for her to produce my elder niece, Jann, one of the most enchanting babies ever to be photographed by Brownie and quite the most fascinating member of the family as she grew up, very like my mother in character and appearance.

John, who spoke fluent French and German, often travelled abroad and returned from one trip foolishly wearing a smart pair of braces obviously embroidered by a feminine admirer. Patricia quite naturally made a great scene and swept back to London with Jann, leaving a private detective to shadow John.

An exceedingly painful divorce followed; by this time he was terrified of Patricia and could only think of ending the entire tragedy, so at the trial he failed to get a ruling from the judge that he must have official access to his daughter. Patricia revealed a somewhat jealous streak because she forbade any member of my family to have any contact with the child, so for some twenty years we all lived in ignorance of each other.

When John died and I had to go through his papers I found a couple of pathetic notes which had been sent by Jann to the office. In the meantime Patricia remarried, a charming man who became a delightful stepfather, and as he had a family of sons by his former wife, the MacDonald household became a relatively happy one, while the Hartly Hodders suffered great pain in their severance from their first grandchild.

John, too, married again. For his second wife he chose a delightful young woman, Pamela Moore, with an equally delightful widowed mother. John and Pamela produced a daughter, Judy, who has inherited the family brains and who is following a successful career on the Stock Exchange. They were happy enough at first but rifts soon appeared in the relationship. Pam played an excellent game of bridge and John was never interested. The strain of the war years had been enormous and he was already suffering from the cancer which was to kill him. My father betrayed him because he had always promised John the chairmanship of the Hartly Hodder firm, but when Father's will was read, it was just as he had written it and signed it the day he married my mother: he had left everything to her. My mother should, in my opinion, have stepped down in John's favour, obviously she had no knowledge of running a shipping firm, but she foolishly presided over all the meetings with John sitting miserably at her side.

John was unable to find anywhere to live so as my father had died in July 1944, we decided to divide 5 Apsley Road into two, with my mother staying in her bedroom with the use of the library, while Gareth and I took over the rest of the house to use as a studio with boarding accommodation for five girls. Half Bristol lay in ruins but I was lucky enough to find a wonderful 'Jack of All Trades', Tom, who with his friend tore off the tarpaulin, put on a new roof and proceeded slowly to redecorate the house from top to bottom – a job he accomplished just before he was cruelly stricken with cancer from which he died.

Nor of course could we find a cook, only dailies in plenty from whose lack of culinary skills we suffered for about a month, when Gareth heard of one who specialised in curries and had lived with her late employer in India for many years. I sent Gareth to interview her and she was delighted to accept the post. This move was particularly sensible of me because she detested women, so throughout her year's sojourn with us Gareth gave her orders and whenever he was in Clifton sweetened her by telling her tales of that wonderful country. Strangely enough, she, poor creature, developed cancer of the liver and died peacefully leaving me to start the search again.

This time I was successful for when I entered Mrs. Hunt's staff agency, I found there a remarkable and efficient lady who had trained with the Duchess of Beaufort, having entered Badminton as a kitchen maid and finished as a lady's maid. We took to each other immediately and, hey presto, a happy relationship was at once established. Florence Gilliard as my housekeeper and friend remained with me for some thirty years, until at the age of 60 she decided sensibly but to my sorrow to retire, for by this time she wasn't at all well. There was nothing she couldn't do: silver and furniture had never been so well polished, never had the household run so smoothly. She tended my mother whenever Mrs. Collins was absent, she managed the flowers beautifully and of course now I could concentrate on my job of creating a school whose excellence I hoped would become a by-word in the world of speech, drama and theatre.

And so, we came to the end of the war absolutely exhausted; there were a number of street parties, nothing in Apsley Road because of course it was too long, and with two main roads at either end there was too much traffic, so we all had individual parties in our own back gardens.

Act 3, Scene 1: The Hartly Hodder School

I made a reputation first as a performer then as a successful teacher, as a result of which I became the youngest examiner for the Guildhall School, in company with such people as Guy Pertwee, Daniel Roberts and Dorothy Dayus. We travelled all over the British Isles, Ireland and occasionally Switzerland.

I founded the Hartly Hodder School of Speech and Drama in 1944 at 5 Apsley Road and with a devoted staff of three, Phyllis Maklin, Christine Lane and Georgie Bodman, we ran a very successful business for some 30 years. I cannot omit the name of dear Graham Harris who ran the Music Department of the School. Husband to Christine, he taught singing to all the students and the piano to those who had any ability.

The specialist subjects on the Diploma course – history of drama, fencing, costume, French, music and singing and dance – were handled by specialists which meant that we had a very large part-time staff. Those who passed were then equipped to win scholarships to a London drama school such as RADA. A famous film actress, Deborah Kerr, sometimes worked with the students. Georgie and Christine both had tiny children, so we set up what must have been one of the first crèches.

We all adored the house which was a very beautiful one, full of family furnishings, with a lovely garden. Gareth had his own sitting room where, after he became ill, he used to give tutorials to those students of ours who wished to take what were then 'O' and 'A' levels. I used the billiard room as my big studio, Christine, now my partner, used what we called the Green Room, the students slept in three of the bedrooms and had their own bathroom and loo on the top floor. I turned the servants' sitting room in the basement into a bedroom, the large kitchen into a make-up and study room with its own machine for making any kind of drink. The cook now had an electric cooker in the scullery, her own bathroom and loo, so every part of the house was used.

We had a number of names for the acting company we started during World War II: at first we called ourselves 'The Forty Four Club' but when 1945 arrived this seemed pointless so we next entitled ourselves 'The

Hartly Hodder Players'. (As we were winning various classes at various eisteddfods, and as I was by now an established examiner and so of course knew practically all the judges, that seemed to give us an unfortunate advantage.) The lion Eric Gill designed for us we then adopted as the mark of the school as well as of the company. One group we called 'The Green Lions' and then as we launched several junior groups – one 'The Red Lions' and another 'The Blue Lions'. Our dear friend, John Gallaugher, artist and designer, was so impressed with this design that he painted the Hodder crest on the centre door of my sideboard, my mother's Oxley crest on the left door, and my personal crest of the lion on the right one.

This was an interesting period in the professional theatre too. This must have been about the time in the late forties that George Robey came to star in the Bristol Hippodrome pantomime; he and Gareth struck up an immediate friendship and we gave several parties for that loveable and vulgar old rascal, a master of timing.

Theatre techniques were again changing for, in 1955, Brecht's *Mother Courage* and Becket's *Waiting for Godot* electrified London audiences. I was particularly excited by *Mother Courage* for it was the first time I had experienced Brecht's particular techniques of mingling tragedy, comedy, musical comedy plus music and songs. This was his own production played in German and never shall I forget the tragic death of the dumb daughter or the indomitable and lonely figure of Mother Courage pulling her wagon up the new revolving stage as the curtain fell.

A long list of my students comes to mind. In 1954 came a most interesting student, Barbara Jefford. Barbara was a star from the start, with a very definite view point. I always remember the first Shakespearean character we were studying and I was laying down the law, when she interrupted saying, "I don't see her in that way at all!" I was amazed for no-one had ever questioned my judgement before, but we discussed the speech and she won and from that day I think I started to become a more interesting teacher for I always began my lessons or classes by encouraging the students to give their opinion and discussing every aspect before anyone started to memorise anything.

Barbara was our first student to win the Leverhulme Scholarship to RADA; while she was there she won the Bancroft Gold Medal, then their premier award. Barbara's successes heralded a wonderful period for our school, an exciting period throughout the 1950s. All the following won similar RADA places: Margaret Whiting, Helene De Crespo, who was smuggled out of Poland as a tiny baby hidden in her mother's muff, Anthea

Morris, who created a stir in the studio by insisting on taking a year out before her final examination and travelled by sea around the world, and Hazel Lewis, the grand-daughter of Arthur Ransome.

I haven't room to mention all the other equally gifted students who won scholarships either to the Guildhall School of Music, the Rose Bruford College or the Webber Douglas School, and all this looked as if it would go on for ever until in 1956 came the production of John Osborne's *Look Back in Anger*. Now the whole picture changed. Sir Kenneth Barnes, the Principal of RADA, had loved our work and would accept anyone who had trained with us because he knew that our approach was a realistic one, that the students would be disciplined and that they had as wide a cultural background as one could provide in three years, also they liked hard work. When Fernald succeeded Barnes we were 'out' and had to start to rebuild a reputation. Life is like that, isn't it? Just as you think that you are at a peak, fate kicks you in the pants – it's all supposed to be character building and I am sure a little adversity is good for us, but not too much.

Talking of adversity, I never had a particularly friendly relationship with Bristol University but in the 1960s we began to use the Winston Hall in the Students' Union building for our productions; a hateful place in those days with a huge gap between footlights and the first row of the stalls. The porters there were all sternly pro-union and at the stroke of 10.30 they went off duty leaving everyone to struggle as best they could. No rehearsal ever finished at the stated time and this led to endless complications and arguments.

I remember on the final day of our last production there curtain down was at 10.15 and somehow all sets, furniture, props and so on had to be out of the building in 15 minutes. This was impossible so we stacked it out of the way marking everything Hartly Hodder and saying that we would pick it up first thing on the following Monday morning. The porters had failed to tell me that another company was coming in as soon as we moved out: they arrived and were of course furious to find so much obstruction, so they dragged everything to the top of the building. When the day porters arrived and found the top floor more or less blocked, they were furious and opened the windows and just threw everything to the ground – you can imagine the dismayed fury when our stage crew arrived to find practically everything smashed. Fortunately we hadn't hired the furniture from the Old Vic but had used things from Apsley Road, but that didn't help us because nothing could be used again and our insurance did not cover this kind of misadventure. I can only describe the affair as an expensive nightmare.

But back to the first ten years: one year we decided to hold a production in the garden because the weather had been wonderful and we thought that nothing could be better than to do a Greek play, and with so many women *The Trojan Women* was the immediate choice. We rehearsed out in the garden and then we realised that if we were on the flat and the audience was on the flat, there wouldn't be much contact between us so I got my stage carpenter to erect a huge wooden edifice with all sorts of levels on it.

First of all we decided that we would put the audience there while we did the play in the garden, then we realised that if were doing an afternoon and later a six o'clock performance, the sun would come through the trees and would hit the eyes of an imprisoned audience who would not like that very much, so we then again changed our mode of attack and decided that we would play on the wooden edifice and leave the audience sitting on the lawn.

That worked excellently because it meant that the wooden staging was a continuation of our back door and of course it made it very easy for entrances and exits. The afternoon performance went marvellously, everyone enjoyed themselves and the audience was most enthusiastic. When the evening people arrived and assembled themselves in the garden, I announced the play by using two of our family coach horns that usually ornamented the hall. They were very difficult to blow, but at least two members of the company managed to achieve these hugely dissonant blasts. Well they blasted and as they blasted the first roll of thunder came and almost before you could breathe, the most enormous storm ensued. Everybody was drenched, so the audience and cast just had to rush into the house or to the garage, wherever they could find any sort of shelter, and I'm afraid that was the end of that performance: I never attempted another outdoor spectacle, although we constantly used the lawn at the back for movement and fencing classes during the summer.

We're now in the late 1950s, when my first beloved partner, Phyllis Macklin, decided to join her husband, Ned Scott, who had by this time become the head of the Electricity Board, in London. So we gave a huge party for her and Donald Adams, that wonderful baritone, consented to give his services. At that time he was the leading singer with D'Oyly Carte but soon after he sang for us, he joined the Covent Garden Opera Company and sang almost every role, not only in this country but all over the world. But at this time, he was considered to be *the* Mikado of the century and he sang that part, arrayed of course in his Mikado costume, with every bit as much fervour and artistry as if he were performing in the Bristol Hippodrome – it was a memorable night.

Phyllis' move to London, where they had a lovely flat and entertained lavishly, had very strange repercussions. She was most kind for it was very convenient to us to have such a base for the students, many of whom had gone to London by now, who were only too thankful to visit Phyllis and Phyllis was only too willing to give them free access to her flat.

One student in particular, Diana Hoddinott, was a great admirer of Phyllis and Phyllis of her to the extent that Phyllis gave her a key to the flat so that Diana could come any time she liked just to do her work, lie down and have a rest, or read. Well, this particular morning Diana came and went straight into the kitchen to make herself a cup of coffee only to find Phyllis prostrate – she had had some terrible attack. Diana rang Ned who in turn rang the ambulance and Phyllis was rushed to hospital where they just managed to save her life. That was a true case of charity beginning at home.

Another dearly loved student was Teng Gee Lee, only daughter of a Chinese millionaire. She was a brilliant mime and quite a good actress who fitted rather surprisingly into our household, making her own bed and washing up the tea things willingly, though she had never before dreamt of performing such menial tasks. Her father gave her a car and the sight of Teng Gee in her scarlet open two-seater was soon familiar as she whizzed through Clifton streets. She celebrated her 21st birthday while with us and we gave a splendid party for her. She even stayed at No.5 through the holidays sometimes, she was so happy to be with us.

One summer I went to Reading for the Federation Summer School where I was taking the Acting course with John Holgate in charge of public speaking and Greta Colston of mime. In those far off days the Speech and Drama section was still the poor relation of the Federation and all the attention was lavished on the musical side, but we certainly enjoyed ourselves mightily.

During this particular week Teng Gee rang to ask to see me on the Sunday of our return, to which request I consented rather grumpily – horror of horrors, she had fallen in love with a penniless Icelandic student and would I please tell her father? For a week I threatened, pleaded, cajoled, while she was adamant. Her father, who could speak no English – and of course I could speak no Chinese – was constantly with an interpreter on the telephone begging me to use my authority.

On the following Monday morning, while he was still speaking to me, she burst into the Green Room and announced that they had got married – by this time she was 23 so there was nothing I could do about it, and off they went. The story has a happy ending: they lived for a while in Iceland where Teng Gee taught mime, then they returned to Singapore with their two children and lived there for a few years, but Jon liked the Singapore climate as little as Teng Gee liked Iceland's, so they agreed amicably to part and he and the children returned to Reykjavik. Eventually the two children married and gave Teng Gee two grandchildren. After her father's death, Teng Gee gave up teaching mime and took over the family business, called Seahorse Balm, which is thriving mightily thanks to her joint efforts with her mother, Datin Lee.

One foreign student didn't fare so well, the daughter of an African king, a most gifted and charming child who wished to teach the subject on her return to her own country. Unfortunately soon after completing her training, she fell in love with a friend of another student's family. They all seemed happy enough and as, again, she was about twenty five, I didn't see any reason to interfere. The young man was quite pleasant and soon they had a flat together. One day she returned in floods of tears, the wedding had been a hoax and he had now fallen in love with another woman, leaving her high and dry as she had quarrelled with her family over the affair. Gareth went to see the man and told him what a swine he was, but what could one do, we comforted her as best we could. She then returned to Africa, after which we never heard from her again.

One of the facts of life I learned from working with so many and with such different types was that when two people adopt a child, that child should always be told of the circumstances. I can think of at least five instances when between the ages of 18 and 21, the student discovered or was told the truth. In every case this came as a dreadful shock and studio work was completely disrupted as we all tried to help the poor child to cope with her altered circumstances; usually they accepted matters in the end, but in one case there was an attempted suicide which fortunately failed but only after the use of a stomach pump. I only wish that parents would tell the truth about their children.

I had another case – an epileptic. Again I was not warned and one day during a movement class I demonstrated how one could fall apparently killing oneself but without doing any damage. It is a very spectacular exercise and one I always enjoyed doing because the blow to the head seemed so realistic. I would then explain the very simple technical means by which this effect was achieved and usually a number would immediately come forward to attempt it, but this time there came a dreadful cry and our poor epileptic had a severe fit.

Well, I knew nothing about such matters; I was terrified by the spectacle and the sounds, but fortunately one of the students had a brother who suffered in a similar fashion and she at once straddled the girl and succeeded in pulling out her tongue from her throat and, with our soothing words and a cup of weak tea, the frenzy abated leaving everyone very shaken for the rest of the day. Of course I telephoned her parents who came to fetch her and only then did they calmly inform me about her illness. The student was a most intelligent young woman and a fine actress but of course she could never follow this career and I am sorry to say that she died young.

Another student had a bizarre background. She was an orphan who had been adopted by her uncle. While the girl was still at school her head-mistress decided to take them all to Madame Tussauds and almost the first spectacle to meet this child's eyes was the model of her mother who had been brutally attacked and killed on a beach. This time the uncle had told me the truth so I was well aware that we might have problems. Perhaps I should never have taken her, but the girl was so pretty, so obviously gifted that I accepted her into the school. In any case, she married happily and had two lovely daughters.

By this time I had established a hierarchy: we had a head girl, a head of house, a librarian and someone to enter telephone calls in a book. The head girl was always my choice and it worked out well. The head of house, the librarian and the telephone girl were less successful, perhaps because they were chosen by the students. By this time the studio was so large that a few rules were essential: punctuality to meals and classes, books from the library to be entered and returned with dates in the appropriate columns, telephone calls to be noted in another book with payments. I simply hadn't the time to cope with all these details and in any case it was obviously better for the students to be given some sort of responsibility. The arrangements worked reasonably well until the 1960s – those were the 'flower power' days – when so many people became irresponsible. For instance, I discovered that my librarian was using valuable books, said by her to be untraceable, as props to keep her bed off the floor. The girl who had to enter the telephone calls never coped with them all and certainly never collected the cash. At this time I managed to get the students affiliated to the University's Students Union so that they could enjoy the many festivities and facilities there. I was especially pleased about this as we were always suffering a ratio of five girls to one male, so it seemed a good opportunity to encourage them to develop new relationships, but, although I never realised it, the drug problem was just beginning.

MR HARTLEY HODDER.

BRISTOL MAN MADE DANISH KNIGHT.

Honour For Mr Hartly Hodder.

Bristolians generally, and especially those interested in the shipping and Consular business of the port, will be interested to learn that the King of Denmark has conferred a high distinction upon Mr C. Hartly Hodder, senior partner in the firm of James and Hodder, ship owners and ship brokers, of Queen's Square, Bristol.

In the official intimation which has reached Mr. Hodder it is stated: "The Chancellor of his Royal Majesty's Orders of Knighthood makes hereby known that it has graciously pleased His Majesty as by rescript the 30th May, 1902, to appoint another Vice-Consul in Bristol, Mr. Clement Hartly Hodder to be Knight of the Dannebrog Order. This is signed Harald Prince of Denmark.

The honour is a rare one, only three others of similar rank are held in England, and Mr. Hodder, who has represented Denmark as Vice-Consul for nearly 20 years, is naturally greatly pleased, although the distinction came as a complete surprise.

The decoration which is worn by members of the Order, is a very handsome gold pendant, the Maltese Cross in enamel being surmounted by the Royal monogram, and crown in solid gold. Mr Hodder, who has taken a big part in the public life of Bristol as city councillor, president of the Shipowners' Association, and Chartered Shipbrokers, chairman of the Bristol Maritime Board, and many other offices, will receive many congratulations.

BRISTOL

IN SCHUBERT'S TIME

LECTURE IN GERMAN AND A CONCERT

FROM OUR OWN CORRESPONDENT

BRISTOL, Saturday.

On Thursday, the German Consul, Sir Hartley Hodder, presided at the first concert given by the Society of the University, and addressing the audience he drew their attention to the literary and commercial value of German. The interest felt in this language in Bristol was proved by the large audience who gathered in the reception room of the University.

The meeting began with a lecture in German by Dr. August Closs, M.A., Head of the German Department, on "Vienna's literary circle at the time of Schubert." The lecture was illustrated by lantern-slides. It dealt chiefly with those men and women who made their contribution to the literary and musical life of Vienna.

The feature of the evening, however, was a piano and violin recital given by Mrs. Travers and Mrs. Norman (Miss Desiree Aimes). The programme consisted of a Mozart sonata, a Beethoven sonata and a Duo by Schubert. The piano, a Bosendorfer concert grand, was the gift of one of Bristol's benefactors, and this was the first public occasion on which it was played.

Colonel Lister, one of the Society's most helpful and stalwart supporters, expressed his thanks on behalf of the audience.

Eileen's father was a leading figure in the Bristol business world.

BRISTOL DRAMA CLUB

— presents —

"To What Red Hell"

A Drama of two families, by Percy Robinson.

"For None can tell to what Red Hell
His sightless soul may stray."
—*The Ballad of Reading Gaol.*

WEDNESDAY AND THURSDAY,
January 28th and 29th, at 8 o'clock.

CLUB DRAMA.—Miss Eileen Hartly-Hodder as Madge in the Bristol Drama Club's production of "To What Red Hell."

Bristol Drama Club, 1931.

BRISTOL DRAMA CLUB.—Tense moment in the play "To What Red Hell," at Victoria Rooms, Bristol, to-night.

X

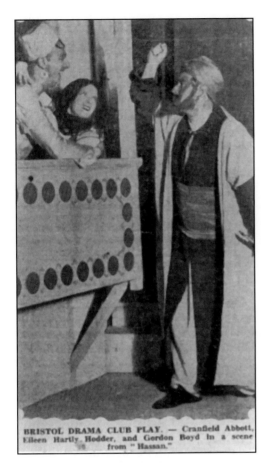

BRISTOL DRAMA CLUB PLAY. — Cranfield Abbott,
Eileen Hartly Hodder, and Gordon Boyd in a scene
from "Hassan."

Hedley Goodall's notable production of
Hassan, in which Eileen played Yasmin.

"Hassan"

I UNDERSTAND there is some intensive
rehearsing in progress at the present
time in connection with the production of
"Hassan," which the Bristol Drama Club
intend offering to the public at the
Victoria Rooms for the nights of January
28, 29, and 30.

Great as has been the ambition of the
B.D.C. in the past, they have never
attempted anything quite so magnificent
as this present endeavour, and the
measure of its success has been keenly
anticipated by amateurs throughout the
West of England.

There is a particularly large cast, not
only of actors and actresses, but of chorus
singers, of music makers, and of dancers,
the chief persons being Gordon W. Boyd,
as Hassan; Eileen Hartly Hodder as
Yasmin; Fleming Spence, as Haroun-ar-
Raschid; Nancy Tricks as Pervaneh, and
Maurice Bascombe as Rafi.

EILEEN HARTLY HODDER as Yasmin
in the forthcoming Bristol Drama Club
production of "Hassan."

XI

Amateurs' Triumph In "Hamlet"

From Our Own Correspondent

Hedley Goodall's production of *Hamlet* set a new standard in Bristol's amateur theatre.

BRISTOL, Tuesday.

LAERTES falling to his death from a platform after a staircase duel; a boy taking the part of the Player Queen as in Elizabethan days; a funeral procession in front of an apron stage. . . . . These were among the surprises of Bristol Drama Club's production of "Hamlet" at the Victoria Rooms here tonight.

The sceptical might well ask how an amateur cast, even if it were nearly 100 strong, could hope to give a moving version of Shakespeare's profoundest tragedy.

As a matter of fact, they did all that and more. Apart from the tendency of some of the players to take the verse at too great a speed, the performance, in intelligent grasp of the text and total effect, got very near professional standards.

It may well be that Mr. Hedley Goodall's sensitive and modulated characterisation of Hamlet was due to his being young enough to feel the pressure of the doubt and confusion of our own times.

He was essentially the graceful, meditative Prince in whom excess of thought has paralysed action. Though at times he was too low in key, particularly in the assumption of madness, the various facets of Hamlet's character—the vacillating avenger, the devoted friend of Horatio, the lover of Ophelia—were stamped with truth.

The unmasking of the king was managed with impassioned zest; tenderness was fused with bitterness in the upbraiding of the Queen and the parting with Ophelia Mr. Goodall's quiet expressive delivery brought out the cadence of the soliloquies.

WELL SUPPORTED

Eileen Vaughan played Ophelia with a delicate touch. Her acting in the mad scene was moving in its wistful pathos.

There was a measured breadth about Albert G. William's Claudius, and he suggested well the stirring of the King's conscience. Mr. Cyril Roberts and Mr. Colston Ball were excellent as the two gravediggers, supplying antithesis of mellowed rusticity and pointed simpleness.

The Polonius of Mr. Cyril N. Thomas has the surface quality of sententiousness, but restricted tone robbed it of depth.

BOY AS PLAYER QUEEN

In the lesser roles Mr. Alec Abbott conveyed fantastic grace to Osric, the period fop, while Master Murray Case was a refreshing Player Queen, quaintly stylised.

The rich vibrant voice of Brian Yates made his Ghost convincing, Eileen Hartly-Hodder as the Queen, Graham Corner as Horatio, Hugh Pritchard as Laertes, Edgar Harrison and John Gibson all fitted into the general picture.

Mr. Hedley Goodall has produced the play with imagination and taste. Examples of this are in the silhouetted figures set under the battlement archway against the night sky, the groupings in the players' scene where the rush of the crowd holds the climax.

Professional enterprises might have learned a thing or two from the artistically designed costumes of Francisca Millar. Robes of green, grey, gold, mauve and blue trace scintillating colour patterns.

Much of the emotional atmosphere of the play is due to the three primary colour lighting effects directed by Gordon Holden and J. F. Strachan.

XII

Eileen's mime plays, including *The Enchanted Garden*, were enjoyed by thousands.

CARNIVAL PRODUCTION. — Miss Edith Schwalm as the Prince and Miss Molly Case as the Infanta, during the production of "The Birthday of the Infanta," at the Midsummer Carnival in Bristol.

MASKS IN BRISTOL MIME PLAY

'The Enchanted Garden' At Zoo Fete

Many people responsible for alfresco entertainments in and around Bristol this summer are getting anxious as to whether the glorious sunshine will last, or suddenly peter out and upset some very perfect plans.

A particularly appealing entertainment (writes H.S.S.) is "The Enchanted Garden,' a play in mime composed and produced by Eileen Hartly Hodder, at the Zoo Fete from June 20 to 23.

The enchanted garden belongs to a giant who has forbidden the children to enter.

They find their way in, and play until the giant comes and drives them out and sets two spirits of fire to guard the gate.

But the flowers and the trees wither through sorrow at the absence of the children until the spirit of the pool lets them in again, and the giant relents.

The cast will be composed of students of Miss Hartly Hodder, with the exception of Mr. Bobby Dixon, who will play the part of the Spirit of Fear.

For the giant and the Spirit of Fear, masks have been designed by the Mac Bean of MacBean, who lectured recently at the Clifton Arts Club.

It is believed that this is the first occasion on which such masks have been used in any Bristol production.

Miss Christine Davis has executed the costumes.

＊　　　＊　　　＊

I WROTE recently about the stage masks made by the MacBean of MacBean, which were demonstrated to members of Clifton Arts Club.

Well, Miss Hartly-Hodder has achieved a personal triumph in persuading the master mask-maker to design masks for the giant and the spirit of fear who are appearing in her new mime.

Forbidden Garden

SHE tells me that it is the first time that such masks will have been used in a Bristol production.

One of them will be worn by Bobby Dixon, who will be the spirit of fear.

Mr. Dixon was the deformed dwarf in "The Birthday of the Infanta," which was seen by more than 2,000 spectators at the Zoo last summer.

The rest of the players will be students of Miss Hartly-Hodder.

＊　　　＊　　　＊

"THE Enchanted Garden," she tells me, "belongs to a giant who has forbidden the children to enter. They find their way in and play, until the giant comes and drives them out, setting two spirits of fire to guard the gate.

"But the flowers and the trees wither through sorrow at the absence of the children, until the spirit of the pool lets them in again and the giant relents."

Eileen Hartly-Hodder has a flair for open-air productions. "The Enchanted Garden" should be worth seeing.

XIII

Douglas Cleverdon, photographed by
Brownie Methven-Brownlee.

Eric Gill self-portrait.

Douglas Cleverdon's antiquarian bookshop with Eric Gill's noted
fascia board was destroyed in the Bristol blitzes.

Eileen.

XV

John.

XVI

Gareth.

XVII

Niece Jann, photographed by
Brownie Methven-Brownlee.

Niece Judy on her
wedding day.

XVIII

With godson Simon Mallitte.

Carolyn Harman.

XIX

The 1982 *Evening Post* Rose Bowl adjudicators with Walter Hawkins. *From left* John Coe, Barbara Macrae, Rex Holdsworth, Ula Rigg, John Oxley and Eileen. *Below* From the 1977 report.

The Evening Post Rose Bowl Adjudicators review the past year.....

EILEEN HARTLY HODDER (Hon G.S.M., L.R.A.M., L.G.S.M. (Speech and Drama), Examiner, Adjudicator & Producer.

On the whole the choice of play has not been very exciting and one would like to see a wider range of more original and more adventurous work. It is splendid to have had a Shakespeare play, because this means that the company must have been stretched to its utmost limits, and any group that attempts the immensely difficult "The Importance of Being Earnest" should also be congratulated — few amateur producers or actors have the sense of style so necessary in any period work.

The Stothert & Pitt Drama Group nearly always make a clever choice that suits their material and this year's "The Militants" was no exception. They had an imaginative and solidly constructed set which was very effective and there was excellent team work throughout. Headley Players - still "in the round" - and the St. Ursula's Players have again given great pleasure to their very large following and to their adjudicators. There are half a dozen groups in and around Bristol who always choose interesting material, whose sets are imaginative and well handled and whose playing is integrated and lively - there is no doubt that many producers and players are taking advantage of the various courses run in the city and one hopes, too, that the consistent encouragement given by "The Evening Post" bears the valuable fruit which it deserves.

A number choose to do farce - always a dangerous undertaking for an amateur group, who seldom have the technical ability to establish and sustain the necessary pace. The audience must never have time to think.

There were one or two "bit" parts which should be noted - the Telephone Man in "Barefoot in the Park", presented with satisfactory American accents by the Mercury Players, and the Bishop in "I'll Get My Man", the offering by Downend Dramatic Society.

BARBARA MACRAE (Hon G.S.M., L.R.A.M., L.G.S.M. (Speech and Drama), Examiner, Adjudicator & Producer)

One felt that many of this year's plays had been chosen for economic reasons - one set, modern dress, and a box office "cert". While one is bound to sympathise with this approach, it does limit the opportunities. One exception in the productions I have visited was Freshford Music & Drama Group's presentation of "The Merchant of Venice". The settings were simple, modern dress was worn and the only costumes which appeared expensive were the casket holders' and they were superb. Could other societies think along these lines?

It has been interesting to visit productions of original plays. Timsbury Theatre Group with "Command Performance" and the Winterbourne Players with "None so Blind" were both written with an appreciation of character and situation although in very different styles. Would that there were more entries under this category.

The impression that the 1976-77 season left with me is one of well rehearsed and well presented productions. The day when it is assumed "it will be alright on the night" seems thankfully over.

XX

BACK IN THE WEST: WEIRFIELD SCHOOL'S MOST FAMOUS OLD GIRL ...

IT IS now nearly 40 years since Bristol drama teacher Eileen Hartly Hodder had a promising young pupil called Barbara Jefford.

Eileen, who still adjudicates for the Evening Post Rose Bowl competition, certainly had the magic touch as far as Barbara was concerned.

For, after a spell at the Royal Academy of Dramatic Arts, Barbara started her auspicious career as a great classical actress by becoming The Royal Shakespeare Company's youngest first lady, opposite Sir John Gielgud.

"I can't praise Eileen enough," Barbara said in Bath this week, where she is appearing in the Ira Levin chiller, Rosemary's Room.

"She taught me verse-speaking and what she taught me was invaluable. I still hear her voice when I am doing things on stage and she helped me to respond to what I think are my strengths and my limitations."

Barbara made her name in classical theatre with the big companies, playing with luminaries like Gielgud, Redgrave, Quayle, Mitchell and O'Toole.

Surprisingly, this is the first time she has toured with a small company.

The teacher Barbara will never forget

"It is very important that we take good theatre around the country," she said. "I have done it with the big companies but this is the first time with a four-hander like this. It means that I am on stage practically the whole time.

"I wouldn't say it is preferable: it is different."

Barbara has not specialised in classical theatre for some time, possibly because of the lack of roles for women in the gap between the young heroines and the grande dames.

"There aren't many good roles for middle-aged ladies. I have been lucky — I have done three Cleopatras, the nurse in Romeo and Mistress Quickly.

"I have yet to do Volumnia in Coriolanus or the Countess in Alls Well that Ends Well, although I have recorded it for radio.

"I have no idea how my career will progress from one thing to another. I did my stint with the big companies and I don't get engaged for three years on the trot any more. I like to keep things flexible.

"I have been devoted to making a career out of chances that come up."

One of her great pleasures recently was to film with the gifted Italian director Fellini in E la Nava Va (And the Ship Sails On).

"Fellini is a wonderful director and a marvellous character," she said. "It was marvellous to be chosen by him and to work with him.

"I have been to see things in the theatre with him but I don't think he would ever want to be a theatre director. For him, cinema is larger than theatre, which it probably is."

Barbara, who was educated at Taunton's Weirfield School and was the youngest person to be awarded the OBE, has played several memorable seasons with Bristol Old Vic.

She was in a televised version of Tess of the D'Urbervilles to celebrate the opening of the Wenvoe transmitter and toured South America with the company in Hedda Gabler and the Taming of the Shrew in 1971.

Her last appearance with Bev was in 1975 in Shaw's Heartbreak House.

Horror

She agrees that Veronica's Room, a psychological horror story, is a departure from her usual material.

"I haven't been through the card with Agatha Christie, not even in rep," she said. "Doing an Ira Levin play has been a different experience.

"He writes so well and so differently. The story line is convoluted and complicated but he has a wonderful ear for dialogue and there are marvellous parts.

"Audiences find it gripping because it isn't a whodunnit with a detective. Everything just unfolds in front of you, and it is not a moment too long.

"But in that short amount of time, Levin has said everything possible."

Barbara Jefford, one of Eileen's many former students with fond memories.

Diana Hoddinott with husband Harry Towb.

Lord Biffen, a former pupil, spoke of Gareth's great influence and love of the English language.

Eileen at work in Apsley Road.

Lallie Hicks' 80th birthday party: ex-students from left to right: Nancy Tricks, Rosie Jacobs, Hope Meredith, Phyllis Smale, Hedley Goodall, Nesta Baker, Barbara Macrae, Margaret Davies.

The first of three 80th birthday lunches, at which Rex Holdsworth's niece, Clare, is seen presenting Eileen with a model of *Arkle*.

I wasn't happy over another unfortunate occurrence. I had a friend with an unruly niece and she begged me to take the girl. She auditioned quite well and settled in quietly enough though she became extremely demanding in class and was always trying to attract my attention and sulked if I ignored her. This attitude became more and more persistent and at last I had to speak to her and explain that in a class everyone was equally important. At this point she produced a knife from her handbag and lunged at me; fortunately my reactions were always very swift and I was able to take evasive action, whereupon she rushed out of the studio and locked herself in the upstairs lavatory.

I knocked gently on the door and asked her to come out, but she shouted that she was swallowing the bottle of Domestos, she wanted to kill herself. At this point someone rang the doctor for me; he came at once and together we persuaded her to open the door. He immediately gave her a jab, having already rung for an ambulance and arranged for her admission to hospital. When the ambulance men arrived she clung to every piece of furniture and had to be forcibly removed, all the time declaring her devotion to me.

I've seldom been so distraught. Of course by this time I had to telephone her aunt and tell her what had happened, whereupon that lady said that she wasn't at all surprised because the girl had previously chased their cook around the kitchen with a carving knife. I felt bitterly – and do so still – that she should have warned me for I would never have accepted the girl had I known. This saga continued for several weeks, the poor creature wept bitterly, asking repeatedly for me; they gave her some sort of drug and finally the aunt begged me to visit her. The doctors agreed with this request, so in great trepidation I drove to the hospital with a doctor and nurse to see her. As soon as we met she clung to me, desperately begging me to take her away. She seemed quite lucid and as I found the place absolutely terrifying, we finally persuaded the hospital to allow her to return to the aunt. Needless to say I could not possibly accept her again and indeed never saw her again as ultimately she was committed to an asylum.

Now let's turn to a more cheerful episode. A young man made an appointment to see me at six o'clock one Monday evening. He arrived early and was shown to the waiting area where several students were chatting. Now let Diana Hoddinott take up the tale: "A couple of us waiting saw him make the mistake of knocking on the hallowed door and go straight in uninvited. A mistake I need hardly say that he made only once." When he reached home he wrote a charming note of apology and asked for another appointment. This time we met and so began a friendship which has lasted warmly for some 50 years.

He was a most interesting young man whose father had been killed in World War I and whose widowed mother was struggling to educate her son. He, Michael, was powerfully built and was working on the railway in spite of a left arm severely affected by polio. Together we worked on his broad Bristol accent and before long he was speaking difficult blank verse passages with great appreciation. I was so impressed by his intelligence that I asked Gareth to undertake his background studies. The two men understood and liked each other immediately and before long Gareth was working not only on English Literature but on Latin. Michael's brilliant brain power enabled him in two years, starting from scratch, to win entry to Oxford where he made his mark and gained a degree. He loved Latin as much as Gareth did and the two often spoke and nearly always wrote to each other in this fascinating language. When he left Oxford, Gareth presented him with a copy of the *Oxford Book of English/Latin Verse*, edited by H. W. Garrod, with this inscription: 'Once the most outstanding and gifted pupil of Gareth Vaughan-Jones'.

My next story is a sad one. A warm-hearted and attractive woman entered her daughter in what was now the Hartly Hodder School. The pretty girl she brought to the audition was gifted but very dark-skinned and obviously not her daughter. As we became more friendly she told me the background: one dark and stormy night, a truly Bronte-esque touch, an intimate friend of hers had rung the bell in a highly emotional state and swiftly blurted out how she and her happily married husband had more or less adopted a black sergeant from the American Army. This man was an exceptional musician, sensitive and most unhappy in wartime Britain, so she and her husband, both musicians, had encouraged him to feel at home and use their grand piano whenever he liked.

One evening he had arrived with news of an immediate move overseas; the husband was away and in a tragic moment the two were making love in the conventional manner on a hearth rug in front of a roaring log fire. He then departed and she wisely decided not to mention the incident ever again. Days went by and she discovered that she was pregnant. Of course the husband was delighted, as well as the families on both sides, and she could only share his joy.

The baby, a white and beautiful girl, duly arrived and the rejoicing among everyone was tremendous but gradually the baby's skin became darker and darker until it was clear that the husband could not be the father and she was forced to acknowledge the whole sad incident. Of course he was devastated, he thought long and hard throughout the day and in the evening he told his wife that he would overlook the whole affair provided that they left the neighbourhood immediately and that the baby would be instantly offered for adoption.

Anguished, she rushed to the only friend she felt she could trust and this splendid woman put on her hat and coat and drove directly to the hospital and removed the infant, later adopting her legally. This infant became the lovely girl and we were so happy to have her. Her work was of a high standard and she was obviously an actress in the making. We did our best to interest her in a teaching career but she was determined to go to London and the stage. Today, she would have found work without doubt for she spoke beautiful English and had a fairly wide range of achievements, but in 1958 it was quite another matter. She failed to find an agent and after a couple of disastrous night club appearances for which she was untrained anyway, she decided to accept the gift of a cottage in her adopted mother's grounds where she has lived ever since.

We had another witty and lovely student who was married with twin daughters and obviously could not go on to RADA because of her domestic commitments, so she joined our staff. The students all adored her because she was so young and such fun. This youthfulness made it rather more difficult for her to remain apart from them and I became a little concerned about the continual gusts of laughter which accompanied many of her lessons. One Monday evening when the day students had left and only our boarders remained rehearsing in the Green Room, the telephone rang and when I answered, June's husband enquired when she was likely to reach home. I replied that I presumed she had left at the usual time, a fact confirmed by my head girl.

The long and short of this story is that she had run away with one of my students, not my favourite young man nor one I considered particularly gifted. It was all extremely traumatic, not only for the poor husband and the children, but for me left high and dry in the middle of the term with a staff vacancy. If she ever reads this, yes, of course, I forgive her, but it was very wrong of her to treat us all so badly and I don't understand how anyone mature could behave so irresponsibly.

I have only one more incident from studio life where I suffered from this selfishness. I had a mature student before the war, not very gifted but a hard worker. Her husband was called up in 1941 and because it was difficult to get good staff, I asked her if she would like to join us to teach the technical side of our training. She accepted with alacrity, telling me that when the war was over she would of course rejoin her husband. This seemed an arrangement suitable to us all. Well, the war ended and in November 1946 her husband was suddenly demobilised. Naturally I expected her to work out the remainder of the term but, no, he arrived back on the Sunday and that evening she telephoned to say that she would not be in again! I simply could not believe that she would behave in such a manner and again I had to call on my long suffering staff to work ever longer hours. At this time, fortunately, I had a most efficient head girl who took over much of the junior work leaving my junior staff free to undertake the technique classes.

Many of the students made unfortunate marriages about that time, they seemed to prefer unsuitable men, like gardeners or grooms with entirely different backgrounds. All of them parted ultimately but several have found better partners the second time round and have settled into happy family life or jobs.

I had another beautiful girl, a Persian, most sensitive and gifted. Unfortunately as soon as she left us she fell in love with an English pilot. Of course her furious father would have no truck with this and he forced her to return to Tehran where she has remained ever since, unhappy and isolated, writing quite lovely poetry. She has an aunt who was lucky enough to escape to the West living in Paris who can occasionally smuggle a letter and even copies of her books to me. I always reply but have no means of knowing if she receives my letters. I think of her so often and know from her letters and poems that she still greatly loves the studio and England.

Another fascinating student came from Minehead where her aunt had been among my original trio of pupils when I started at Weirfield School. She later became quite famous as the original Polly, the barmaid in *The Archers*. She was highly original and sensitive and very close to her father who died while she was in her first year with us. One of my saddest moments occurred when I entered her room a few weeks later and found her quietly crying as she held her father's old pipe to her heart. She was lovely in the house, always helpful and thoughtful; I think the happiest period of her life was when we produced *Razzle Dazzle* by William Saroyan in 1945. The opening number was 'Hello Out There', a tragic arresting little scene. My student played the girl and John, another promising boy, the young man. The two fell blissfully, youthfully in love, but after a most successful run when we all lived in a sort of haze of delight, one Sunday morning John went out to do a job and was killed on his motorbike. I shall never know how we got through those days. It was agony for us all but unspeakable hell for the girl. She never recovered, though many years later she married a brilliant technician in the Bristol Aeroplane Company and when he retired they moved to a remote cottage on the top of a lonely Gloucestershire hill, not the wisest choice of dwelling one would think. I have never heard one word from her since.

A production I greatly enjoyed was *Antigone*. I had a wonderful array of talent at that time; I think we achieved a remarkably high standard. Phyllis Macklin and I again worked together on this agonising and emotional play, and for a change we hired a magnificent set from the Kelvin Players. Again the two young leads fell head over heels in love and when, after the final curtain fell, they asked if they might go off on their own to unwind I consented readily as I thought they both were mature and responsible young things: alas, a couple of months later our Antigone announced that she was pregnant. Her family, rightly, were very distressed, as were we all, but I feel that they wrongly held me entirely responsible for the incident. The young people sensibly never married and it was a courageous act on the part of that 18 year-old child with a promising career ahead to decide to have and to keep the baby. She has since had a very successful business career.

Act 3, Scene 2: Examining

As well as teaching in Bristol, I went on my travels as an examiner. Of all my adventures I think my favourite story is of the first festival I did in Connemara. I'd been given instructions at Belfast where to change trains, so I asked the porter if the train I was about to board was the correct one. "Sure," he said. "They'll be telling you where to change." We chuntered on in beautiful sunshine through wonderful green countryside, finally stopped, and everybody got out. I was still sitting there when the guard came along and said to me, "Would you know where you're going now?" When I explained, he said "Holy Mother of God, this train hasn't run along there for twenty years!"

So I had to get out with all my luggage, there were no taxis, but I found a man with a car that was literally held together with string, rope and wire. I told him I had to be in Connemara by three o'clock and he assured me I had nothing to fear and so in I got. He kept up a wonderful flow of Irish blarney while we dashed through villages and shot over cross-roads: he never stopped, slowed down or blew a horn. In the end I just closed my eyes tightly and prayed. However, we covered the distance in record time and he dumped me at the hotel. As there was nobody there to meet me I decided to walk down to the hall where the festival was to take place. It was all locked and barred and the notices were all in Gaelic, but one seemed to proclaim my name, so I hoped I was in the right place.

My committee turned up about five and said they were ready to start work at six o'clock so "we'd better have a drink first." Competitors came on bicycles and donkeys, in old cars and pony traps, from all over Ireland. It was the most enjoyable and festive occasion. We finished at one o'clock in the morning when the candidates had to return home while the committee took me off to a party.

The festival lasted for three days and on the last night the party was louder, later and more cheerful than ever. If I had had any sense I would not have gone to bed as I was due in London to start examining for Diplomas at 4 o'clock that afternoon, but I felt I must just have a short sleep because I did want to be 'on the ball'. Foolishly I gave the hall porter a splendid tip and asked him to call me at 7 a.m. sharp – I never saw him again and as I woke up so late I had to telephone the Guildhall and explain that I would not be there that day.

I had another nightmare experience in Ireland. Again I had to travel from Belfast to the south, and again I was misdirected. This time I reached a station from which the line had been closed for the past thirty years. Again I found a willing but dangerous driver to take me to the outlying convent where I was to examine. He then spent the day celebrating his uncle's wake so he was more than an hour late picking me up. This time we deserted the roads and instead lurched at once over fields and ditches. I was due to catch the mail train from Dublin to Belfast in order to examine there next day. As we reached a steep embankment an express exploded into view so, clad as I was in a tight skirt and three inch heels, my friend manhandled me into the guard's van, throwing my books and papers after me. Best of all we steamed into Belfast a mere five minutes behind schedule and I had enjoyed a hilarious chat with guard and driver.

Once when I was due to examine in Glasgow, I went by train on the old *Flying Scotsman* – a most fascinating journey with the huge engine, as Auden says, "snorting noisily up and up and up and up the fell", across Shap and finally way down into the station. On this particular occasion we had a blizzard and we finally stopped in a snowdrift. The heating failed, but I had had the foresight to take a rug and I sat with it wrapped round me. I shared the carriage with two men who kept looking longingly at me. I couldn't bear to watch them freeze to death so I finally asked them to share the rug – I was in the middle and had the best of it! One of them was so grateful that he kept on asking the attendant to fetch yet another bottle of champagne and this, together with a delicious luncheon basket, kept up our spirits splendidly.

At long last we were more or less dug out by snow ploughs and off we struggled again; we were almost into Scotland when, bang, we stopped again. The man on my left looked out of the window to see what was happening, while the other one lifted down a square box very carefully and put it on the seat, then politely took down my luggage. The other man turned back from the window grumbling "the signal is against us" and sat down, plonk, crunch – the box contained three dozen new laid eggs.

I eventually reached the boarding house where I was to stay for the course and because I had to be at Jordan Hill College within the hour, the waiter brought me three sardines on a crumpled lettuce leaf, which I gobbled and then asked for the main course as I was in a hurry. "That were the main course," he replied grumpily. Things went on like that. Gareth had been demobilised and came to join me at Jordan Hill where the course was being held. Everywhere was consequently fully booked so I left a piteous message with my landlady to ask if she would allow my husband to share my room. She most reluctantly agreed – at a price I might add – but insisted that we be back in our room by 10.30 p.m. every evening as her husband always bolted the door at that hour. We hated every minute of our stay, hard beds, dreadful food, and to crown it all trams rocketing down the hill with clanging bells all through the night. Whilst I was packing the chambermaid appeared for a tip and said she hoped we'd enjoyed our visit. I replied that we had been pretty wretched on account of Mr. Mackenzie's strictness. "Mr. Mackenzie," she exclaimed, "och ay, he's been deid these ten years."

Act 3, Scene 3: Teaching and Examining

Of course, teaching and examining wasn't all sweetness and light and a couple of painful events come to mind. The first concerned a rather eccentric middle-aged woman who wished to embark on a recital career. She lived in the middle of nowhere in a romantic rose-covered cottage. It was hard work coaching her as she had a very limited range and few ideas when first she started, but gradually her voice and vision developed and she got a couple of engagements. One day she appeared in a state of some excitement: her car had broken down and she had been rescued by a handsome man who became interested in her and started to suggest various poets and dramatists whom she might study. As she subsequently arrived from time to time with very different moves and techniques I felt certain he was discussing her programmes with her, but I was fairly happy about this though some of the material in my opinion was unsuited to her personality. However, at the end of the summer term she invited me to spend a day with her in Bath as her guest to celebrate our enjoyable work together. We lunched at the Theatre Royal and went on to a matinee of a Stoppard play. I told her I would send a card to let her know the date of the winter term and we parted most affectionately. I never heard another word from her, she just vanished into the air and "what seemed corporeal melted as breath into the wind".

The next episode was much more painful. I was taking the drama course at the Federation Summer School in the north of England in the days when the musical side was still paramount. The BBC Head of Music in Scotland was taking the choral work and I was told I must try to involve the choirs in the speech course. We all met for dinner on the opening night and Gareth and the Scotsman immediately hit it off and inevitably went out to a pub afterwards, returning rather the worse for wear.

I decided that choral verse might interest the singers and chose Flecker's *Golden Journey* to *Samarkand* as it had both choral and solo passages. I asked for volunteers and about forty turned up. I distributed the scripts and we arranged to meet on Friday afternoon. Everything went quite smoothly and we were just rehearsing the final line, "We make the golden journey to

Samarkand", when suddenly the door burst open and in marched the wife of the BBC man; she fixed me with a stare so malevolent that I stopped dead in my tracks; she never said a word, just stared. I have no idea why she appeared to hate me so greatly, I can only assume that she held me responsible for her husband's nightly forays with Gareth. Anyhow I found it impossible to continue and I lamely dismissed the class.

Then there were the visits to Stratford. The Society of Teachers of Speech and Drama has been very dear to my heart ever since I joined as a very young member. The STSD decided to make Stratford its headquarters for the annual conferences and there we stayed for eleven happy years. Then, as now, we always found a poet or someone equally distinguished to give the main lecture. I remember one famous occasion when we deputed Gareth to meet our speaker. At three o'clock with an enthusiastic audience filling the hall, the poet lurched unsteadily towards the lectern, leaned upon it and slurred "Any quesh..sh..ions?"

I always encouraged our students to join and certainly whenever possible to attend the conferences. Gareth, John, my mother and I all stayed at the Shakespeare Hotel where we engaged what was then called the Midsummer Night's Dream Suite. We chose this because it had a room large enough to entertain speakers and members.

I remember a couple of incidents connected with our Stratford visits. A new restaurant had been opened outside Bristol so my mother invited us all to dine there on our return. About a dozen of us went, and as the food was very unusual we ordered the most exotic dishes on the menu. My mother who had never paid for a meal in her life had handed Gareth an envelope containing what she thought was the necessary cash; he never thought to open it until the bill was presented to him and when he did he found to his horror that it contained £50 – and the bill came to £300. I hadn't thought to bring any money and he only had enough for the petrol home, but in the end we persuaded the manager to take a cheque.

Another time we returned via Cirencester where a friend of ours had the most beautiful seventeenth-century house complete with blue Wedgwood panels up the staircase. He dined us far too well and we were certainly in no state to drive home, but in those days no one had heard of breathalysing so off we went. I drove ahead as I felt capable of keeping to a steady pace and Gareth in his car was thus forced to keep behind me on the quite narrow roads. At one point there were two roads, one through a town, the other skirting it, so without thinking I took the town route while Gareth went the other way. He was an erratic driver and liked a turn of speed so of course he forged ahead. When we reached the outskirts of Bristol I saw an abandoned car in the middle of the road. I passed it by, leaving it on my right and never thought any more about it. When I reached home there was no Gareth, but I presumed that he had driven our friend Jessica home, so I went to bed. About an hour later there was a call from a hospital to say they had both been injured in the accident but were now comfortable so I wasn't to worry. In the morning, Gareth limped back but Jessica had badly bruised ribs and was detained in hospital for several days. Sad to say that was the end of a very real friendship for she never recovered from the shock and as it was caused by an error of judgement on Gareth's part his insurers refused to pay up – another expensive nightmare.

This delightful Cirencester friend subsequently announced his engagement but then suddenly disappeared. Many years later, Gareth and I went searching for his Welsh property; all we could find was a dirty cottage where he was living filthily. Horrified we turned away and, discussing the matter afterwards, presumed that he had discovered he was homosexual, then a punishable offence.

It must have been about this time that I was asked by the Guildhall School of Music and Drama to undertake their correspondence course. Barbara Macrae helped me to set up the first edition and for a number of years she and I worked together, but as we both became more occupied with our teaching, productions and examining, in the end it was simpler to deal with it alone, so I set up the second edition which we are still using and I have continued to correct papers ever since. I formed a number of friendships with candidates over the years and I expect most of my readers know that witty book *84 Charing Cross Road*, where two people, one a writer from America, the other a bookseller in London, corresponded for many years but never met? I have been luckier for not only have several candidates exchanged letters with me over long periods, they have actually visited me in Clifton, a couple from as far away as Ireland and at least half a dozen from different parts of the United Kingdom. In every case the meetings have proved extremely rewarding and long after the people have concluded the course and gained their Diplomas, I still hear from them occasionally with all their news. I have often learned more from their comments and answers than they have from mine for the course has attracted men and women of exceptionally high mental calibre.

In the meantime, the School had worked happily enough for many years while I was only taking my own hand-picked pupils from Weirfield or Gardenhurst but by now we had become so well known that various local authorities from as far away as Shropshire and Essex were giving us grants to take anyone recommended who had passed our entrance requirements. This of course meant that I seldom knew the background of new applicants and had to rely on intuition and first impressions.

From the 1960s No.5 ceased to be the happy place we had known for the past twenty-odd years for the students started first to drink and then to take drugs. There was one dreadful Saturday night when we had all been to the Theatre Royal as usual and I returned to answer a ring at the bell to find two police officers, a man and a woman, who said they had a search warrant as they had reason to believe that someone in the house was selling drugs, and so she was – I was shocked beyond words. In my favour I must make it clear that the signs of early drug taking and drunkenness are very similar.

I immediately decided to close the boarding school and asked the parents concerned to remove their children. With one exception they sympathised with me and supported my action, the one exception threatened to sue me for negligence, which would of course have certainly ruined the school, but in the end my dear cousin, Sir Denys Hicks, after taking Counsel's advice, managed to buy him off – most expensive.

Fortunately it was the end of the school year, and we were just coming up to summer examinations, so with the help of the remaining parents, we rearranged our timetables for the next few days and our results were as satisfactory as ever. Indeed Nigel Dodd, already a composer and fine musician, won the silver medal awarded by the Guildhall in those days to the student with the second highest marks at Diploma level in the United Kingdom.

At this stage, 1970, I had received a wonderful offer for the house, but I had promised my younger niece, Judy, that she should be married from No.5 that August. We rushed around painting white everything shabby looking, while one of my friends, Mary Newman, did the most lovely flower arrangements everywhere. Judy was given away by her uncle, Sir John Eardley-Wilmot, to Gerard Walker Smith and I am thankful to say that they are still happily together in 1998 and that Judy has a brilliant career on the Stock Exchange. (A professional friend of ours offered to take the photographs but unfortunately, shortly after the ceremony, he eloped with his lover, so we never got them, only the proofs and not all of those.)

Still, we didn't sell the house, deciding that we needed a few more Christmas parties and we certainly enjoyed the next one when an old army friend of Gareth's, Patrick O'Donovan, Foreign Correspondent of *The*

Observer, arrived in high spirits and immediately counted the Christmas cards which I had slung along the staircase walls, there were nearly a thousand of them, and he wrote an article about them and us in his next column. Then in 1972 fate stepped in with the oil crisis, we ran on oil and we knew we could not afford the doubling of our household expenses nor the rewiring of the entire building for electricity – but now no bidders, of course. However, there was no alternative but to move.

Act 4, Scene 1: A New Home – and Sorrow

I finally sold No.5 to a single buyer who happened to have £30,000 in cash and, as no-one else made any offer, my cousin, Denys, advised me to accept, which I did very unwillingly. Now it was difficult to find a suitable flat. I looked at dozens each one dirtier and less attractive than the last. Finally we settled on No.19 Apsley Road. I had to pay £18,500 for it and when I installed a lovely picture window in the sitting room there went another £2,000.

I can't tell you the agony of trying to stuff five floors into one. Fortunately my two nieces both wanted family furniture and portraits and I sold what none of us needed. It was a dreadfully cold and wet January day when we finally moved. I put the removal out to contract, the first estimate was for £2,000, the second £1,000, and because by now I was bedevilled by a shortage of cash we accepted foolishly the lower figure.

The men were unbelievably inefficient – they could not get my beautiful walnut and mahogany wardrobes up the sharply angled staircase, the Broadwood grand piano which they had roped and assured me they could pull through the new window, steadfastly remained stuck in the sodden ground.

Leonardo, our cat, was yowling in his basket and you know what a row an angry Siamese can generate, while Gareth and I veered from despair to sorrow. At last it was over and we sank exhausted, with large brandies and a wonderful picnic basket thoughtfully provided by a dear friend, on to the settee. What we couldn't cram into the flat we stacked in the garage and even then had to give away dozens of books and records. I have read somewhere that to move house is the most traumatic experience in one's life apart from losing one's child or partner and I can vouch for the truth of that statement.

As the removers had to return the wardrobes to No.5, I then had to order built-in wardrobes with sliding doors, two in the spare room, two in our bedroom and another couple with shelves in the kitchen. So as you can see there was now little of the £30,000 left and I was thankful to restart my busy life of examining, adjudicating and teaching. I chose about a dozen

"Behind the Curtain"

by Eileen Hartly-Hodder

The Bristol Playgoers Club

It has been said that a professional actor is a compound of angel and devil and an amateur actor is a compound of business man, husband and father. Perhaps that explains partly why the latter will never create the magic of the former, no matter how hard he strives. Certainly in Bristol there are many who *do* strive!

Since the 1900s, inspired by the genius of such women as Miss Horniman (who built the Abbey Theatre, Dublin and whose repertory company was known as the Manchester School) and Miss Bayliss (founder of both the Old Vic and Sadler's Wells), local solicitors, schoolmasters, printers and doctors, with their wives, met to read, study and discuss the new playwrights. Before long, they founded a club under the leadership of Dr Barclay Baron — The Bristol Playgoers Club — intended to introduce unusual plays to a wider audience with a policy to read, rather than to perform them.

The 1914 war interrupted this vision. But as soon as life returned to normal, the enthusiasts re-formed the Playgoers, and several other lively clubs were founded. By the 1930s, the best were attempting ambitious plays with sets and costumes designed by their own members. Some of you may remember fine productions by the Bristol Shakespeare Society, and the triumphant "Hamlet" and "Hassan" of Hedley Goodall's Bristol Drama Club. Then — 1939 — disaster again! A few brave folk struggled through those hateful years, taking productions all over the area to camps and schools, but the standard of acting and presentation inevitably fell. However by 1950 the amateurs were up and about again. The Bristol Guild of Players was formed: they took the Theatre Royal for a week, inviting a well-known professional director to adjudicate the six plays selected for the competition. But there were now those who, wanting star parts, founded smaller clubs, often presenting only the Esther McCracken type of domestic comedy; though in the midst of this lazy sea of comfort we find a few steady rocks like the Kelvin Players, and occasionally there was an exciting new eruption. One of these was St Ursula's Players.

Spotlight on St Ursula's Players

The Club was formed from a handful of schoolgirls in 1954 under the presidency of Barbara MacRae, whose work for youth is known from John o'Groats to Land's End and beyond to Hong Kong. Marie O'Sullivan became honorary secretary and her husband, Hedley, stage manager. Between them they recruited an enthusiastic bunch dedicated to the group. They even painted scenery in the school field when times were really tough! For ten years they battled, without workshop or rehearsal room, but staging works of the calibre of "This Happy Breed" and "The Heiress". Then in 1960 they found a studio, where they built up their backstage crew and gradually grew into the "ensemble" company of today. Six members have spent over twenty years with the club and another couple of dozen ten or more; by choice there are only thirty-five in the company with a permanent back-up team of seven — how's that for loyalty and dedication? Forced to leave "home" four times in unforeseen circumstances, they're now, with their usual enthusiasm, transforming a dilapidated scout hut into a studio and workshop.

They deserve their success — it has come in concrete form with over seventy awards and in intangible form with the commitment of their members. Their range is wide: from "She Stoops . . ." to "The Devil's Disciple" and, most daring, to "Front Page". Where eight telephones of 1920 vintage were needed for the news room in this play the problem was solved by Hedley, who made seven copies from a genuine model.

Eileen writing on drama in the local press.

91

very promising male and female students of whom Philip Thrupp turned out to be the most brilliant. He had a first-class brain, a splendid memory and an enormous capacity for work; he passed every examination with reasonably good marks, all the time reading widely and consolidating his background.

At this point I wrote to Leslie Fletcher, the Examinations Secretary at The Guildhall School of Music and Drama suggesting that they might like to consider him as an examiner, a letter to which I had no reply. In the meantime as LAMDA, the rival school, was running an interesting summer course, I suggested that Philip should apply for it, he was accepted and while actually on the course, the LAMDA Principal approached him and asked if he could work with them. Philip accepted and in a very short time he became one of their chief examiners travelling all over the United Kingdom and as far as America and Sri Lanka, now with a newly designated title – International Examination Co-ordinator.

To return to No.5, the people who bought our beloved house didn't really care for it, actually it was far too large for a couple whose children were about to leave home, but thankfully the Fergusons, the second purchasers treasure it almost as much as I did. They have lavished love and cash on it and turned it back into the beautiful home it once was. Indeed the garden is now greatly improved for they have landscaped it.

The one thing to cheer us when we arrived at No.19 was a splendid gift from Ann Malone – a TV set on an elegant black stand. We had never bothered to buy a set, enjoying, as I still do, a good radio programme. I remember our first serial was Galsworthy's *Forsyte Saga*, beautifully photographed and performed. It was so enjoyable that Sunday evenings became sacrosanct, we wouldn't have missed an instalment. Another and very different programme later was the satirical *That Was The Week That Was* directed by Ned Sherrin, enormous fun, as was *Yes, Minister* and *Yes, Prime Minister*. Oh, and I mustn't forget the immortal *Dad's Army*, still often revived to my delight.

My dear Georgie Bodman, who had joined the School with Phyllis Macklin and Christine Lane, now took over my Somerset connection. She is a wonderful director of musicals, which she stages in Weston-super-Mare's attractive Little Theatre. She writes her own scripts, adapting stories like *The Railway Children*, she has wonderful support at Rosholm School where her Head and staff supply all her needs. The theatre is very well equipped, with an excellent switchboard, while the professional electrician there is delighted to work for her. Georgie, as everyone calls her, is far more adventurous than I and has taken a course in computers and apparently been christened 'Granny Internet'. Warm-hearted and intelligent she has a splendid relationship with the young and it is wonderful to know that our standards of work and behaviour still prevail.

As far as I was concerned, I wasn't travelling so frequently or widely by now because I was increasingly concerned at Gareth's ill-health, but I became a frequent Rose Bowl Adjudicator and still enjoyed my teaching and Guildhall work, also I took up bridge with great enthusiasm and often played far into the night.

(The Rose Bowl is an amazing institution, first dreamt up by Walter Hawkins, editor and owner of the *Bristol Evening Post*. His drama critic, John Coe, threw himself into it with enthusiasm, joining forces with John Cochrane, a musical comedy expert; Barbara Macrae and John Oxley for the musicals, and myself, were all employed as adjudicators. Walter spoilt us splendidly, marvellous dinners in the *Post's* private rooms, baskets of flowers for the women thanks to Barbara Weeks who became our first PRO, bottles of whisky for the men. All this pampering caused much jealousy and after Walter retired and died his widow, Joan Hawkins, made herself financially responsible for the running of the operation. She wisely appointed a chairman and committee and worked out a set of rules. The whole project has grown hugely allowing all clubs to enjoy the prestige and access to every kind of festivity.)

Of course I was still going every week to our famous old Theatre Royal where the standard of work was good if not as exciting as when players of the calibre of Peter O'Toole and Dorothy Reynolds delighted us. Rodney West in immaculate DJ welcomed us warmly and bade us farewell graciously; but I now watched TV avidly, savouring the range of such giants as Maggie Smith, Edith Evans and Billie Whitelaw, probably the greatest of them all. Never shall I forget her bleakly extraordinary performance in Beckett's *Mouth*. I write of actresses only here not because I am a feminist, for indeed I am strongly unsympathetic towards that movement, but because I have earlier mentioned some of the greatest actors of the century. I really love the theatre and can appreciate the finer points of good acting whether on stage, film, TV or radio. It was also very exciting because hardly an evening passed without my seeing a familiar 'Hartly Hodder' face. I must acknowledge Lyn Farleigh here for she spoke so highly of our training to Sheridan Morley that he thereafter referred to me as "the legendary Eileen Hartly Hodder".

To return to our readjustment of life after the move, it was again a snowy winter and one day I had to lunch at the Savile Ladies Club. I told

Gareth that I would go on to the hairdresser afterwards. After the lunch I came out to find that I was hemmed in and spent the next 40 minutes exhaustedly trying to manoeuvre the car out. I can't imagine why I didn't just walk round to the hairdresser which was only ten minutes away, but no, I doggedly stuck inside the car getting more and more frustrated and exhausted with every tiny backward or forward movement.

At last I emerged and suddenly I had one of those strange attacks of amnesia that I had during the war. I had no idea where I was, I drove up Blackboy Hill and went round and round and round the Downs, I don't know how many times I went round. At last something told me that there was no point in continuing to travel like this, so I went down and turned into No.5. Again something told me that was the wrong place, so I backed and finally ended up at No.19. Gareth met me and said, "Why haven't you been to the hairdresser?" and with that I snapped out of it and said, "I don't know." So he said, "Well, all I know is that your hairdresser telephoned me about quarter past three to ask if you were coming to take your 3 o'clock appointment, and I told him 'Yes'." So of course all I could do was to ring and apologise for my apparent rudeness. That, thank goodness, is the last time I had one of those strange attacks.

Act 4, Scene 2: Family Matters

Now I must backtrack a little to bring things up to date on family matters.

After the war, Gareth had to find a job, so armed with tributes he answered an advertisement from the headmaster of Dr. Morgan's School at Bridgwater, a Dr. Trenchard, brother of the famous airman, Lord Trenchard. Gareth and Trenchard instantly became buddies and Gareth at last found his true niche as a wonderful teacher and an inspiration to all who knew him. That charm, that brilliance, that warm-heartedness endeared him to all and sundry and those years in Bridgwater were probably the happiest of his life.

Unfortunately, one evening, returning by train, he was as usual immersed in books and papers, when he realised that he was at Temple Meads and hurriedly leaving the carriage missed his footing on the narrow board and fell between the carriage and the platform, breaking his ankle. He was taken to Casualty at the General Hospital and returned next day to Apsley Road where it became clear that he had an infection. Suffice to say here that owing to a blunder on the part of the surgeon he developed one of those dreadful hospital infections and an open wound which refused to heal. It persisted for the rest of his life, causing him to take early retirement from the school, a fact which had pleasant repercussions for me as he instantly took over the teaching of English to my own students.

My students usually adored him though a couple of the less intelligent were rather in awe of that penetrating wit. He had many great successes among his pupils at Bridgwater, one of the most outstanding being John (later Lord) Biffen, the Member of Parliament for Oswestry and at one time in the Cabinet and a Privy Councillor until his gentle but penetrating sarcasm was directed against Mrs. Thatcher, who instantly dismissed him like a truant schoolboy. John became a great friend and I will let him speak for himself in the tribute he paid to Gareth on radio in *Desert Island Discs*:

> I remember a wet lunchtime at school when Gareth Vaughan-Jones entertained us by introducing us to music. This is why I enjoy 'Peter and the Wolf'. Not only because of the music but because it reminds me of a particular man who was a great influence, especially when he began to teach me to have an affection for the

English language. Something I have found of great value in my political career.

I always used to tease Gareth and say that he had three topics of conversation: Oxford, India and the War. Quite untrue of course because he was a brilliant talker on every subject. Perhaps he spoke his own epitaph when he said that "I was as at home in an Oxford Common Room as I was in the Barrack Room."

Gareth was a devoted and brilliant companion and for much of our time together we were supremely happy but alas his heavy drinking often made life impossible – it was like being married to a schizophrenic for when drunk he became another man, even in appearance. He would sometimes go for a month drinking just an aperitif before dinner and wine with the meal but then he would meet one of those 'dear old friends', usually in The Naval Volunteer in King Street, with Peter O'Toole as one of his companions, all of whom would offer him gin at once, and that was the end since he would consume a bottle in half an hour and then another, then another and would go on in this way sometimes for days. He usually limited these orgies to the weekends as he generally had enough wit to stay more or less sober for Bridgwater and teaching. He never had a hangover, he would arrive home at 4 o'clock in the morning completely drunk, but at 6 o'clock he would be blithely singing hymns in the china pantry while polishing the silver.

(I think it is a great mistake for people not to learn from having hangovers. I learned very early not to drink much because when I drink without eating or if I drink more than say four or five glasses of anything, I just get sick and that is so revolting and so unpleasant that I have only been drunk once – that was quite enough for me.)

My mother was still a great influence in my life, we were devoted to each other. At first she preferred my brother John but found herself more and more dependent on me and to a lesser extent on Gareth. When we consented to share the house it was at first very easy because Gareth was away teaching, I was often away, but John and Pamela never looked after her as I think they should have done. Pamela was perhaps jealous of her – I think that is a frequent feeling between mother-in-law and daughter-in-law. I must say that jealousy is an emotion that I have never understood but I have seen it destroy so many relationships. It is an emotion one should try to conquer, but I suppose it is like all one's genes, if you are a jealous person you probably can't overcome that particular emotion.

By this time matters were also worsening between John and Pamela, he did such foolish things. I remember he bought a job lot of dark green paint – most unattractive in any case – in order to have the office repainted. Pamela was away for the weekend and when she returned she found to her horror that he had also had the kitchen and hall of their flat done with this hideous colour.

In 1945, he had met the lady who was to become his third wife, Maureen. Desperately ill, he had taken a flat in Weston, leaving the office and the rest of us ignorant of his whereabouts. As no one was now in control of the office I finally discovered his address and went to find him, the door being opened to me by a very pregnant woman. Back we went to the hospital where the surgeon, a great friend, told me frankly that John only had a few weeks to live – where was he to go? He couldn't manage the steps to his flat so would I take him at No.5? I explained that I was running a large business and household and already had an invalid mother, but as there was no hospital that would take a terminally ill patient I was more or less forced into accepting this abominable situation, and then ensued one of the most painful periods of my life, only made possible by the promise of our doctor that he would end John's life when the tensions became intolerable.

They occupied my one spare room. All my staff had liked Pamela, who was a lady though sometimes a difficult one, and they refused to work with Maureen, who to her credit offered to help with all household chores. Dear 'Digger' Knight, his wartime second-in-command, came in every day to spend time with John and to carry out any errands he needed. Pamela was rightly angry with my mother and me and never understood why we consented to house John and his mistress. Poor little Judy, their daughter, was shattered, she adored John and was too young to understand the situation. I now understand why Pamela refused to divorce John, because of course she would have lost all her pension rights.

My mother solved the situation by settling some money on Pamela and Judy, who decided to live in London near all Pamela's relations. With her income assured, Pamela now consented to divorce, and John and Digger paved the way for his third marriage. We had a number of macabre parties hosted by John from his increasingly painful bed. One day Digger and the ambulance men took John and Maureen to the Register Office to be married, with only Digger and Jack King in attendance. A few weeks later Maureen gave birth to a daughter, Anne.

Gareth detested Maureen and insisted that as soon as the baby was born they should live with her family in the Midlands, but by this time John was in perpetual agony so I spoke to our doctor friend and recalled his promise, so that morning he gave John an injection and he died instantly. Needless to say the two of us have never met or spoken to each other since, because of course he could never forgive me for forcing him to break his oath. John was so well known that with Digger's help, I was happy to arrange a huge memorial service in St. Mary Redcliffe.

My mother's condition worsened and I decided to move her down to the library which had a large bow window looking out into the garden, where I felt she would be happier, as she could be part of the establishment. With her nurse, Mrs. Collins, the telephone and a constant flow of visitors, I hope she was as happy as one can be when old and unwell. We moved most of the bookcases into the cloakroom and brought in some of the interesting furniture. The room always looked bright and was always full of flowers and Mrs. Collins kept her beautifully, always dressing her in pale pink.

Rather than leave Mother alone, either Gareth and I stayed in to play bridge or look after her, or if we went out, we tended to take her because although she was an only child she never liked being alone. This constant feeling of having his mother-in-law with him whenever we went to the theatre or a concert or out to dinner became an irritant to Gareth and perhaps was one of the reasons he took to drinking so much.

At this time, as Gareth and I were now both based in Bristol, I bought him his longed-for Siamese cat. My mother, who said she preferred dogs, insisted that Leonardo must never be allowed on her bed, but within two days the kitten was found asleep there after lunch, a habit he pursued for the rest of her life. Our friends teased us about the cat's name which was part of his pedigree, he had 18 champions in this document and he really was a superb creature. He was very much a V-J admirer, who suffered few other humans, indeed he sometimes snarled and even spat at certain of our friends who ventured to touch him or pick him up. The well-known animal artist, Marjorie Wilding, painted him, but failed utterly to catch his essential character. I commissioned her to paint the animal as a present to Gareth who was at that time very ill. I suggested that she took some photographs of him, whereupon she replied very haughtily that she had painted every animal in Smart's Circus and had always been recognised and welcomed by all.

However, Leonardo was different. At first sight he rushed underneath an attractive Chinese stand that we had on the staircase, glaring at her from underneath it and no amount of praise or kind words would make him

Charity champ's medal joy

Eileen's life-long work for the RNLI.

Gold honour for veteran lifeboat lady

RECITAL AT CLIFTON PARISH HALL.

In Aid of Royal National Lifeboat Institution.

A recital in aid of the funds of the Royal National Lifeboat Institution was given last evening at the Clifton Parish Hall by Eileen Hartley Hodder, assisted by Hedley Goodall, Beryl Tichbon, and Norman Jones.

It had been arranged by the Bristol Women's Guild of the Lifeboat Institution, the hon. secretary of which is Mrs Hartley Hodder, and enthusiastic efforts by the guild has resulted in some £300 being raised annually for the cause.

Beryl Tichbon and Norman Jones have achieved success by their two-piano recitals in London and Bristol, and last night they played a series of numbers of varied interest and considerable brilliance.

Eileen Hartley Hodder, gave a most entertaining and artistic series of English verse, old and new, and original sketches, and with Hedley Goodall, the well-known Bristol producer, presented the fairy tale of the Scottish border, called " The Return," by Gordon Bottomley. With a dimly lighted stage and appropriate characterisation the performance was carried out with a realism that added considerably to the reputation of both performers.

A VETERAN Bristol charity worker has been presented with a top award.

Eileen Vaughan-Jones was given a gold badge by the Duke of Kent at a special lifeboat institution ceremony in London.

The dedicated RNLI volunteer, of Apsley Road, Clifton, has helped organise balls, flag days, children's parties and other events since she was a girl.

Amazing

And the award is extra special for Mrs Vaughan-Jones — because her own mother received it in the 1940s.

Mrs Vaughan-Jones said: "I was very pleased but absolutely amazed.

"I've done an enormous amount of work but with the committee.

"Our annual ball used to be one of the highlights of Clifton society.

"The RNLI lifeboat men are wonderful — they go out in their own time for no money and often for no thanks."

move, so she finally had to have a few photographs and even then she never found him in a good mood. He usually sat elegantly with his tail curled very delicately close around his body, but when she painted him he had his tail stretched out stiffly at the back of him, so it didn't look at all like Leonardo. When I gave the portrait to Gareth, he took one look at it, said "That's not Leonardo," and thrust it back into my arms. Well I wasn't going to waste all that money, so I framed the sketches and hung them on the dining room wall.

With John dead and my mother seriously ill I was forced to become chairman of the Hartly Hodder company and I was happy because a shipping friend Jack King, had consented to buy the business and to keep all the staff, but no sooner had this arrangement been finalised than he died from a heart attack and again I was forced to consider the future. This time the Stevenson firm took over, although they were more interested in stevedoring than shipping. But again, as they were willing to take over the entire staff, it seemed the sensible thing to do.

I can remember one amusing incident soon after we had amalgamated. It had become the fashion to arrange mediaeval banquets, so, to Gareth's disgust, the old firm, which had always had homely whist parties at No.5, embarked in car and coach to a nearby castle for such an evening. I was prepared to enter into the spirit of the thing, it was very amusing really, but Gareth was at his most surly. When we reached the venue we were supposed to take on the roles of Lord and Lady of the Manor, and to host the occasion. As Gareth refused to utter a word I had to undertake the task, sitting on the main throne and welcoming all the guests. I have rarely spent a more embarrassing evening. Shortly afterwards the Stevensons bought me out and I have continued to be very friendly with the younger members of the family for we all played bridge regularly together, a pastime I continued until I was taken ill. Circumstances have completely changed over the years and neither of the original firms still exists, but Roger Stevenson has continued to help and encourage me in every possible way.

In those days I worked hard on various committees ending as chairman of Bristol Conservative West Women for three years, a task I could never have sustained had it not been for my wonderful Party secretary, Mrs. Linda Johnson, who always whispered the correct answers to me. She knew the rule book backwards. I suppose I must have been reasonably efficient for when I resigned in 1974 the members gave me a magnificent black leather handbag and had my portrait painted in pastels by Marjorie Wilding.

My mother eventually died in 1971 after a long illness borne uncomplainingly. She was greatly loved and I received over 700 letters, many of them so touching that I felt I must reply personally, but you can't just scribble, "Thank you so much, best wishes". So after I had struggled with the first 100 I was driven to use a printed acknowledgement which ended with a slight variation of Bunyan's famous lines, "All the trumpets sounded for her on the other side". Among her papers I found a most moving acknowledgement of my care for her, in which she wrote: "You have been a most wonderful daughter and I am sure you will be rewarded for the happiness you have given me". Death duties were horrendous and Gareth and I should have sold No.5 immediately.

Act 4, Scene 3: Gareth's Death

Gareth's death in 1982 was one of the most bizarre happenings in my life. He had a strange condition whereby he could suddenly drop down as if he were dead and I remember that we were at a party at The Savages one night and suddenly somebody called from the other side of the room, "Eileen, come quickly, I'm afraid Gareth has been taken seriously ill." I rushed over of course and there he was lying on the ground, apparently dead. Everybody was gazing in horror when suddenly he opened his eyes and got up. We were all shattered and somebody rang for the ambulance. In those days ambulance men took you where you wanted, so they took him back to the flat and I put him to bed and he was perfectly all right. When I talked to him about the incident, he said that it had happened to him once before when he was at Oxford.

Well, that was hopefully the end of it and we went on with our lives, and then he became very ill after the fall from the railway train. One evening we had our supper and went into the sitting room to listen to the news and we were sitting side by side when suddenly he gave a sort of 'click' and when I looked at him I saw that he had left me. Well of course I immediately rang the doctor – in those happy days when you rang they were most upset and came instantly. So one came and pronounced him dead and sent for the ambulance; the ambulance men came and also pronounced him dead. The doctor decided that the best thing would be to take him to the hospital at Ham Green. We drew up at the hospital and when the ambulance man opened the door, Gareth was sitting bolt upright!

When everybody had recovered from the shock, Gareth was put straight to bed where I left him sleeping. In the vestibule the night nurse had spread an enormous sheet of paper on the table and insisted that I went through, not Gareth's medical history because of course I didn't know it, but my own, back to my grandparents – I can't think why! I signed this document and as Gareth was apparently sound asleep, I went back to the flat to look after Leonardo. The next morning I thought it's no good arriving at 9 o'clock, they'll be changing night and day staff, so I'll arrive there at 10, which I did, walking straight into the ward where I had left him. But he wasn't there, so of course I rushed to reception and said, "Where is Mr. Vaughan-Jones?" and they said, "We decided we will take him back to the Infirmary because he must be operated on immediately."

I then burst out in my most authoritarian voice and said, "He will not go back to that hospital. We have both had the most frightful experiences there; if there is any nursing to be done I'll have him back at our flat and look after him there." By this time the doctors had arrived and you know how in those days they used to stride through the ward with all the nurses fanning out behind them – I broke all the rules by rushing through the nurses and seizing the doctor, saying "I'm Mrs. Vaughan-Jones, Mrs. Vaughan-Jones, I will not allow my husband to go back to the Infirmary, if he is going anywhere he will come back to our flat."

The doctor was furious with me and said it was completely unprofessional, I couldn't possibly cope with him because he was so very ill and I said, "Well either you keep him here or I insist on taking him back." So they then put him in a little side room which I thought was very kind of them. (It wasn't kind of them at all because apparently they always do that when you are going to die – but I didn't know that.)

It was an extraordinary experience being in this little room with the door open between it and the big ward because from all over the ward in varying minor or angry tones people were calling, "Nurse, nurse" and the nurses took not the faintest notice: they were all sitting round a table at the end of the ward, roaring with laughter and chattering away. Finally I saw a man get out of his bed and you know how they have these little bottles – one for water and another for urine – well I was quite horrified when he did not pick up the water bottle, but the urine bottle of another patient, and drank from it. . . .

At that point my authoritarian tones came back again and I bellowed "Nurse", the sound reverberating round the whole ward, and this time of course the nurse came up and I told her what had happened. She didn't seem to be at all perturbed, anyhow she did go and deal with the patient. We were there for a few days; I must say they were very kind because they put a comfortable chair in this room and they wanted me to stay there all night but Gareth doted on his cat and it would have made his last hours unspeakably unhappy if I had stayed with him and not returned to look after Leonardo, so back I had to go and pet and feed and pamper the cat, perhaps for an hour or so and then I would drive back to the hospital early the next morning.

Then one night, probably about five nights later, while I was doing the same routine, Gareth died. The hospital rang me first thing in the morning and asked me to go in but I said "No". There was no point in seeing him. However eventually I had to go. The late Barbara and Val Davies arrived some two hours later – it is extraordinary how quickly news gets round – and took me to the hospital and the Registrar to complete all the necessary forms. It was a great help to have them there because they could tell me exactly what I had to say and do and helped me make the arrangements for his cremation.

This was the first time I'd ever seen anyone cremated and I thought it was a loathsome service. We went to Canford Crematorium and there were all sorts of pink and white walls, pastel shades which I detested. As Gareth was an atheist there was no point in having any sort of service, so we managed to get hold of someone, I've forgotten who, just to say the committal words. Only his sister, her husband and I were present. I don't think I was crying because I'd cried so many times while he was ill, it had been an agonising two and a half years. It had been very gradual because he would say to me "Eileen, I'm so sorry I can't take the cat litter down," and so I'd take it down and have a little cry, a little weep, and then perhaps two days later he'd say, "Oh, Eileen I'm terribly sorry, I can't take the rubbish down," so I'd go off and take the rubbish down and come back and have my little weep. So there were no tears left when he did die.

I returned to the empty flat and Leonardo seemed to know what had happened because although he'd always rushed to Gareth to be picked up, he now rushed to me and got into bed with me. About a week later I could see that he was ill because he couldn't jump up on my bed, so I telephoned the vet who came at once and said, "I'm afraid he's got kidney trouble, I'll give him an injection and if the injection works it will be all right, but if the injection hasn't worked when I come tomorrow morning, I'm afraid I shall have to put him down." Needless to say I spent a miserable day; Leonardo was obviously very ill, he was sick and didn't want to eat, couldn't even keep water down, and when the vet arrived next morning it was quite clear that he was dying, so I held him in my arms, the vet gave him an injection and he died immediately.

So in 1983 my life had to continue sans husband, lover, and cat.

Act 5: Living Alone

It wasn't easy, I had spent my whole life surrounded by family, students and friends. Well, of course, my wonderful friends telephoned me or visited me every day. I was still lucky enough to have a few very promising students so I still had a raison d'être, especially as the Rose Bowl was steadily growing in importance and my bridge now developed into a major pastime. I took to playing at weekends and any free afternoons. My friends in the country, the Brearleys, Diana Grant, Dorothy Lucas and others made tremendous efforts to involve me whenever I had an available moment.

The Brearleys was a particularly happy arrangement; Douglas would pick me up on his way from the office, arriving at his home we would have a drink and settle down to a couple of rubbers before dinner. His wife, Joy, is a superb cook and together they make wonderful hosts, so what more could one desire? A beautiful house with immaculately polished furniture and silver, the meal a gourmet's delight, with all the vegetables and fruit grown and served straight from the garden, superb wines served in exquisite glasses, coffee and every kind of liqueur, and then back to the bridge table until 2 or 3 in the morning. Up, not with the lark, but with a tap on the door from Douglas about 7.45, then with quite a rush, bath, pack, breakfast and off in the car, as Douglas liked to be in his office by 9.30. He would drop me off on the way so I just had time to read my correspondence by 10 o'clock when, if necessary, my very dear ex-student and secretary, Joan Seaward, would be ready to deal with anything that needed doing. I often stayed with the Brearleys or Diane White and other friends and relations and I always hated to return to an empty flat.

But after the first couple of months, I wasn't really called on to live a lonely life. I was extraordinarily lucky still to have the loving support of Sarah Fernandes, my nieces, their families and the many ex-students who had become my friends. Work, too, again proved a great panacea for I had constantly to read plays and critical assessments in order to keep up to date. But in 1983 bleak thoughts of a possible lonely Christmas and birthday loomed, only to be quickly dispersed by my dear friends Linda and Stuart Tyfield who invited me to join their house party: there were twenty guests with four or five languages spoken.

Linda, brilliant and beautiful, is at Bristol University in charge of genetic research, on which subject she has lectured all over Europe, Canada and the United States. The next day was my birthday which I claimed to be my 75th but which was really my 80th. As it was Brian's birthday on the Sunday we decided to make a weekend of it. He and Jann arrived soon after tea on the Saturday just as I was receiving an annoying message from my cleaning lady's husband to say that she had gone down with 'flu. Frustrated I collapsed at the news but within minutes came another ring at the bell and Carolyn and Michael Harman turned up bearing a large bottle of champagne and a beautiful bouquet from The Playgoers Club. On hearing my news they instantly said that they would deal with everything for me. Haven't I got wonderful friends? Michael wanted to return as a Kissogram boy but I didn't feel Brian would approve, he was already looking slightly askance at Michael's sarong, for the Harmans were on their way to an ethnic party. Anyhow a little later my dear godson Simon and the Tyfields appeared and we all sat down to eat the lasagne which Odette de la Cour, my downstairs neighbour, had cooked for us, finishing with a good port and a splendid cheese board. Carolyn and Michael not only washed up but managed to put everything away more or less correctly, they then joined us for coffee, brandy and wonderful French chocolates before going on their way to eat curry with their friends.

And so to bed as I had to be up early-ish to greet the family for lunch. David, Sarah and Iain arrived first, closely followed by Andrew and his wife, Angela, all laden with gifts including wonderful food, smoked salmon, chicken in a tasty sauce of asparagus and mushrooms, a huge cheese board and a lemon flavoured birthday cake with soft icing and a token number of candles, blown out by Brian and me in one joint puff. Tired out by all the laughter, I fell sound asleep in the sitting room. Joan Seaward turned up next morning to help me put the spare room ready for Doris Hart who was due to spend the weekend with me. During her visit, off we went to the pantomime at the Theatre Royal. It was a real family affair, full of local jokes and illusions with much audience participation.

Of course over the years I went continually to my dear old Theatre Royal and whenever I could I now watched plays on television avidly. By this time hardly an evening went by without seeing a Hartly Hodder name, Penny

Beaumont, Pam Ruddock, Nicholas Le Prevost, Joanne Pearce and Lynn Farleigh, among others.

So 1983 was a year of parties. The local members of the STSD arranged a special recital as a tribute to my long association with them. It was held at Blue Lodge, the lovely home of Janet Tuckett. Many members came including dear Hedley and Roger Jeffery, the latter such a brave man to make an appearance suffering as he was a great pain. Unknown to me Jean Howell had asked one of her daughters to inscribe in exquisite calligraphy all the selections in a beautiful leather book – of course now I wished that I had chosen different poems but it was too late to change the programme.

Philip arranged the music to reflect the mood of each poem and the readers were Rex Holdsworth, Jean Howell, Philip Thrupp, Lynn Barnes, Wendy Nasmyth, Rena McMahon, Janet Tuckett, Barbara Smith, Ula Rigg and Rosemary Powell. This memorable occasion was greatly enjoyed by us all, though I found it a highly emotional experience because Rachel Blundell made such a charmingly appreciative speech about me. Most people have to wait until they are dead before the world is told how greatly they are loved, I am indeed blessed to have had that tribute plus two others in that same year.

The next party was arranged by Joy Hedges. This wasn't altogether a joyous occasion as Joy had chosen St. Valentine's Day, the anniversary of the day when Gareth had officially proposed to me, and, as he hadn't long been dead, it was again a very emotional affair. I was greeted by the Lady Mayoress of Bristol and it was all rather formal with speeches and a presentation of a superbly crafted 'Arkle', the famous racehorse. I shall always be grateful to Joy for such a magnificent occasion. That same year I was awarded my Gold Medal by the Duke of Kent, President of the RNLI.

Another party held in 1989 was a truly joyous affair. It was organised by Pat Parry-Jones at Ann Malone's beautiful house where over a hundred ex-students met to eat, drink and remember old times. Pat had invited my nieces and their husbands so it was an incredibly happy day. Diana Hoddinott, who came with her husband Harry Towb, made a marvellous speech about the work and worth of the studio referring to us all as a 'formidable pride of green lions'. Pamela Allcock presented me with an attractive picture of No.5; she had painted it and all those present signed on the back. The picture still hangs facing me, frequently admired.

107

Frank and Linda Webber's 90th birthday greeting.

For getting around at this time I had a staid white Hillman Hunter, very different from the glamorous Lagondas, Sunbeams, Rileys and Bentleys I had driven in the past. My brother John and I used to drive round Brands Hatch where we met the famous Bentley Boys. I shall never forget the frisson up one's spine as the speedometer for the first time touched 100.

I was most unfortunate with my last Bentley; for fun I used to start in top gear – probably bad for the engine – at the bottom of Shute Shelve in Somerset and would be roaring at 70 at the top of the hill. There I always checked because the road dropped quite steeply at that point and in any case there was an unseen lay-by on the left. One day an old cousin, Betty Newling, who lived near the cottage at Nether Stowey made famous by Coleridge and Wordsworth, wished to return home and as I was busy I asked my chauffeur to take her back. He was a brilliant driver, always sober, so I never mentioned this particular hazard, with the result that he tore up and over the hill just as a Mini pulled out from the lay-by. To avoid hitting it Phillips had to swerve across the road and literally wrapped the car around a great oak tree! Of course he had to report this to me and I am ashamed to say that I exclaimed, "Not my Bentley!" and forgot to enquire about his well-being. I am such a fool and without Gareth to prompt me I had continued to pay the full insurance instead of lowering it each year for depreciation, so I only got the current value of the Bentley and the Hillman was the only car I could afford.

And this is why I gave up driving. Rex Holdsworth telephoned me in great distress to tell me that his wife had walked out on him, taking most of their furniture with her. Handsome and warm hearted, Rex is a professional actor, excelling in light comedy; he and I have worked and played together for many years. As I drove up to see him I considered whether in spite of our age gap I would suggest that he came down to No.19 to stay with me, at any rate for a time, but when I reached the house I discovered that he couldn't cook either, so I never made the offer, very wisely as it turned out for he soon met a very dear lady to whom he is happily married. She, by the way, is an excellent cook.

On my way back I had a near miss with the car and decided that I would give up driving. I am sure that everyone over 85 should have another thorough test in town, motorway and Highway Code. Expensive, of course, but at least it would give some much needed employment. It was maddening to be car-less especially as I had had one since my 16th birthday, but I was recommended to a delightful Irishman, Mr. Baugh, who looked after me with courtesy and care. By this time I needed this for I had developed some infuriating weakness in my right leg which necessitated medical care.

There was more sorrow to come. Douglas Cleverdon had come to stay in August 1987, an idyllic few days though I was sad to see how frail he looked, but the old spirit of appreciation was there as he enjoyed the new Susie Cooper dinner service and I handled his gift of a fragile small Chinese bowl. Now fate struck again and at 3 a.m. one morning later that year his daughter Julia rang to tell me of his gentle death. I was completely stricken, suddenly afraid of the darkness, the loneliness. I telephoned Philip who came around immediately and talked quietly and sympathetically until I felt I could face the world again. I had wonderful letters from Julia and from Douglas' widow, Nest, who had both understood our relationship and whose continuing friendship has helped me through the last years. Douglas was a warm hearted man, a brilliant companion and in my opinion one of the finest members of the team who presented the BBC's famous Features Department. I am blessed indeed to have enjoyed his love.

Because of my weak leg I was given an attractive ebony and silver walking stick with instructions that I must use it at all times. So I became rather more housebound, though I still felt able to cope with a couple of adult students and was able to continue with my Guildhall correspondence course from which I had developed several rewarding friendships and of course I continued to play bridge.

One day I was expecting Georgie Bodman to lunch and went without the stick to rinse my hands, the bell rang and I turned sharply to answer it and fell heavily and painfully. Georgie was marvellous, she realised from my position that I had probably broken something so set about telephoning ambulance and hospital and accompanied me to Southmead where I had an immediate operation on my right hip. This was my first experience of the National Health: the surgeon put me in a small ward with five others. It was interesting because the woman on my right was a gypsy and could neither read nor write, she had had no idea that she was ill but when she was tested they discovered that she had a serious liver complaint. She was evidently very well off because marvellous gifts were brought to her every day.

Opposite me were two delightful young women who also had broken legs – we had had a sudden freeze early that morning – but they too were found to be suffering from far more serious conditions. There was a strange lady who attempted to get out of bed every time she was put in, and she fell the moment she put foot to ground; she was a source of endless trouble to the staff. The last inhabitant was someone who never spoke nor moved during my stay. I received hundreds of 'get well' cards which were strung all round the ward. The staff thought I must be a film star!

After a week I was put in a very pleasant private ward where there were two Sisters in charge, both very efficient and kind. Unfortunately, I then had a thrombosis so was put back into a general ward and given a blood transfusion. Later I was returned to No.19 with a resident nurse for a fortnight, apparently they expected me to die, but before long I was leading quite an ordinary life apart from paying a small amount to have most efficient remedial home care.

The only thing I really disliked at Southmead was when the male nurse had to give me a bed pan. Otherwise I almost enjoyed this fortnight and certainly the food was good. Back home I picked up the threads of life again and apart from using a Zimmer from time to time I was reasonably mobile. So mobile that I could stay in various places including the home of my niece Jann, where she and her family had created a special garden for

110

me, which I formally opened by cutting a purple ribbon. It was great fun to be with them, they are a remarkable family, typical Hodders in that they are all workaholics and very creative.

When I returned home my leg started to give me further trouble, my doctor prescribed Warfarin and the district nurse arrived each week to take a blood sample, very unpleasant; this was analysed and the dose increased from time to time, while I struggled against a loss of appetite and consequent weakness. Sarah Fernandes became seriously alarmed at my condition and when I asked her to stay the night with me she felt certain that all was not well and telephoned the doctor and, although it was Christmas Eve, he persuaded the General to give me their last bed. I was met there by a splendid doctor who gave me an instant blood transfusion thereby saving my life for a second time. They were very good to me but the food was abominable and I lost whatever appetite I had had, but somehow they rehabilitated me sufficiently for Jann, Judy and Simon to persuade Stokeleigh to take me.

Now my life changed again and I hope for the last time. Jann, Simon and Sarah had the unenviable task of clearing the flat, not only of furniture and paintings but of all the silver, china, books, ornaments, jewellery and clothes, plus hundreds of papers. I am afraid I am a hoarder and although I thought I had stripped No.5 of the contents, I had still kept an alarming number of possessions. Of course it was again difficult because I was moving from quite a large home to a single room.

Weighing only five stone, I was too ill to concern myself with decision-making and I can't thank my friends enough, and those three particularly, together with neighbours Odette de la Cour and Elizabeth Eddy for coping with things on my behalf for days. It would have been easier to sell everything but they rightly decided that I wouldn't wish that, so I allowed the family to buy the furniture very cheaply while the silver, tea and dinner services and jewellery I gave to Jann and Judy, keeping half a dozen of the best pieces for my room.

On January 7th, 1997, while I was still in a state of shock and weighing only five stone, the ambulance men carried me from the General Hospital and placed me on the hardest, lumpiest single bed imaginable. Mercifully I was met by Gella, a wonderfully sensitive carer, who comforted me until Simon and cousin Sarah arrived. In the meantime, however, they had taken my remaining possessions to Stokeleigh and it was a great relief to be greeted by these familiar objects on the walls – family photographs, my Chinese vases and the French balloon clock, the bookcase filled and my

111

Louis XVIth chair in position. This chair by the way still has its original horsehair in the seat. I can picture one of my great-great Oxley ancestors using a family fan or quizzing glass thereon. My 'cell' as I call my roughly 14 × 21 foot room, thankfully includes my own washbasin, loo and hanging cupboard. Next day, Linda Tyfield arrived with a night light because I had become terrified of the dark. The Hibbs, Georgie, Joan Hawkins, Diana Towb, Joan Seaward, Cecily, Jackie, Carolyn, and others arrived within days, bringing comfort and love, and sometimes very welcome cheques.

Family and friends visited and telephoned unceasingly but I found it impossible to settle or even to eat. At this point Elizabeth Eddy spoke severely with me asking me if I was really intent on starving myself to death. I still continued to suffer from sleeplessness and nightmares so Ruth, one of those efficient ladies running the home, put me, albeit unwillingly, on sleeping pills, so that as I found that I calmed down and had no ill effects when called each morning for 8 o'clock breakfast, I have continued the habit. Simon installed two telephones, one by my bedside, the other by an armchair, looking out on trees and a lovely green lawn, dear Margaret and Peter Hibbs sorted out my wardrobe for me, taking my summer goods to their own home until I needed them, and making arrangements to sell any designer-labelled evening regalia as obviously I no longer needed these. Margaret has worked unceasingly and has got excellent prices, even selling a couple of beautiful 1930s outfits at Christies.

I must record the odd coincidence of my collapse and that of Christine Lane. Christine and I had worked splendidly and happily together for some fifty years and when I finally closed the studio she joined the staff of Badminton School where, as Mrs. Harris, she made another successful career for herself. She was a dynamic teacher, full of energy and always prepared her background with the utmost care but she worked in a Svengali manner, it's very successful but a method of which I disapprove. Anyhow, I collapsed on the Friday night and she, while teaching at Badminton, collapsed on the Monday. (Unfortunately she died some six months later, while I am lucky enough to be struggling on and even working again.) Not only did Christine collapse on the Monday, but my dear Joan Seaward was unmercifully mugged on the Tuesday, receiving such shocking injuries that she never recovered and died a year later.

Epilogue: Curtain Down

All my life I have been surrounded with good luck and the love of friends, but as this odious century draws to a close with all its frightening wars and 'isms' and appalling scientific discoveries, while like the Gadarene swine we rush to destruction, I look back into the kaleidoscope of my existence and recall memories, sometimes tiny, sometimes huge.

The gentle touch of the pink cherry blossom as I swing under that great tree at Middleton House, the sting of the wind in my face as I learn how to handle a boat, the exciting discovery of ancient ruins all over Dartmoor and the subsequent deeper knowledge of the great cultures of Greece, France and Italy, the miracle of Armstrong's journey to the moon, the joy of a lark-filled sky while returning from a Lifeboat Ball with godson Paul, all Gloucestershire sparkling beneath us, making love with Douglas in that pink tamarisk-fringed meadow by a blue Cornish sea, the terror and black misery of most of World War II.

Brilliant memories of railway journeys in Europe and the UK, the excitement of certain theatrical experiences, starting with Coward's *Vortex* and that performance of *Journey's End* which precipitated the chasm between my father and me which sadly we never bridged. The tingling excitement of my first *Petroushka*, my incredible reaction at first reading *Tess of the D'Urbervilles*, and strangely enough later when reading Wilder's *Bridge of San Luis Rey*. I can never pass beneath my adored Clifton Suspension Bridge without recalling that tragedy.

Innumerable Stratford experiences, the huge lovely crimson carpet suddenly filling the enormous stage as Julius Caesar made his first entrance, Barbara Jefford's 'Portia', gathering her voluminous peach-coloured skirts and calling "Therefore haste away" to Nerissa, as they journeyed to Venice, John Neville's gentle Hamlet at Bristol Old Vic, Adrian Noble's enchanting production of *The Dream* at Stratford, which I last visited with Linda and Frank Webber, that touching moment in Coward's *Cavalcade* when the honeymoon couple moved away leaving the word 'Titanic' glowing on the lifebelt. My own Ann Malone's heartbreak playing of Hester in *Deep Blue Sea*, the beauty of Vivien Leigh in *Skin of Our Teeth* at Bristol Hippodrome. My introduction to Shakespeare, thanks to Miss Arbuthnot-Lane, a lasting benefit – my only one from Clifton High School. The Dior 'New Look'.

Those days of joy walking with Gareth in the country, picking great bunches of velvety cowslips or smelling bluebells in a Somerset wood, picnicking with him by the lily pond at Kingsweston House, the home of the Napier Miles. Poignant scenes as we moved from No.5 and as I watched him gradually disintegrate, worst of all holding our Prince of Cats in my arms after he had been given a lethal injection. Remembering gambling parties of the 1930s, with Johnny Marks dancing on the dining table, miraculously avoiding the cut glass and antique silver, while declaiming 'The Shooting of Dan McGrew' at the top of his voice.

(I must mention here the one courageous act of my life in the 1930s. My father rarely drank to excess but when he did he became violently quarrelsome. One night about 3 a.m. our telephone rang and my mother whispered agitatedly, "Your father has a pistol, please come at once to get it from him." So of course Douglas and I went right over. I told Douglas to keep in the background and when I reached the foot of the stairs, there father was, revolver in hand, pointing directly at me. He bellowed "Get out or I'll shoot you." So I walked swiftly up to him and wrenched the pistol from him so violently that he fell, hitting his head on the banisters. I ignored all this and turned and walked rapidly back to our flat, from where I rang mother to tell her that I had the pistol. None of us ever referred to the matter again.)

I remember Sidmouth one September when out of the mist came a strange noise and an unheard of surprise – an aeroplane, although we didn't know it was an aeroplane, had crashed on the beach and a French aviator staggered from the wreckage. Could it have been Blériot, I often fancied.

In Wales, I remember one journey that we took to a lake in the mountains when bare-footed children cursed us and threw stones at the car as we passed through the village. We reached this calm and beautiful spot, settled ourselves with a picnic and turning a knob on what I believe was called a 'crystal' set, we listened enthralled as the magic of Beethoven and Mozart floated on the breeze. Nowadays we take all these sounds for granted but it was a miracle then.

In 1924 Douglas and I went to Greece and were overwhelmed with the majesty and imagination of those wonderful buildings. I still can't understand the magic which created the whole civilisation centred on that comparatively tiny city, Athens. One wonderful day we visited the ruined

114

amphitheatre of Epidaurus and there from its centre I spoke Shakespeare's thirty-third sonnet in a completely natural way – the words reached Douglas far away on the perimeter. I know that those impressions fed me strongly especially when Christine and I produced *Antigone* many years later. I think it was one of our best productions, certainly it was the most emotional and demanding of plays. During that period I read all the translations then available.

Still a long time ago, I remember two holidays. In the hot summer of 1928 I was attending a lecture in London and seated myself under an open window. During the lecture someone opened the door on the opposite side and I was conscious of sitting in a draught, however there was nothing I could do about it. I caught the train home and by the evening was feeling quite dreadful. Douglas had arranged to drive Brownie and Edith Schwalm down to Cornwall and I was following with another couple in my car. As everybody was dependent on Douglas for transport, although I was feeling dreadfully ill, he had to go off, leaving me alone. I was by the way still in the flat at No. 8. The pain was so excruciating that I fainted dead away and when I recovered and finally staggered to the bathroom and looked at myself I thought I had leprosy all down the side of my face!

I had never heard of shingles but shingles it was. I was dreadfully ill though fortunately the path of the shingles went up into my hair and down my cheek and into my neck, missing my eye. After a time I recovered and Douglas and I thought we must have a few days by the sea in order for me to recuperate. I didn't feel like going to an hotel because I really was still so feeble, so we went to Devon searching for a really quiet abode and as we slowly passed through the narrow lanes we saw a most charming rose-covered cottage with a man outside putting up a notice to say 'Apartments to Let'.

It looked so inviting that we stopped there and had a wonderful welcome, the wife was a beautiful cook and she looked after me for the first week so that I was almost recovered by then. One hot day Douglas and I decided that we would explore so we went to the top of a cliff. It all looked most inviting so down we went splashing through pools, making a great deal of noise and laughter, when suddenly Douglas said "Eileen, those are adders", and lo and behold the pools were full of adders. Of course, we turned tail and scrambled madly up trying to avoid the pools this time and when we got to the top again we saw the notice that we had ignored when we arrived there, 'Danger, Keep Out, Adders'.

115

The second holiday was with Gareth towards the end of World War II. Clough Williams-Ellis, a friend of Gareth from Oxford days had recently opened Portmeirion which was all very new and different then – I imagine it is rather chi-chi now. He had built these darling little different coloured cottages all over the valley, it looked like an Italian village, everything a different colour. The hotel was at the bottom by the sea, you could either stay in the hotel or you could board in one of the little cottages. We decided to take a cottage which was just below the Angelus, so that as neither of us ever seemed to have a watch, at least we would know the time. Our breakfast was brought up to us every morning and we would wander down to have the rest of our meals in the hotel and very good ones they were too! It was there that we saw the first of the great Spanish dancers to come to England, I think his name was Roberto. I remember Clough looking at him longingly as he almost danced out of the door, "what a nice tight little bottom!" As usual it rained for part of the time and so I took to writing letters and articles and Clough arrived one morning and said "Eileen, you'll be interested to know that you are sitting on the very chair and at the very desk where Coward wrote *Blithe Spirit* in three weeks." I don't think Coward inspired me exactly but it was very fascinating to know that the great man had actually stayed there.

Back in the present – I recall the day Barbara Ivey came with a charming bunch of bits and bobs from her garden. She had read an amazing article in the *Daily Telegraph* a few days earlier about a skeleton which had stood in a case for many years outside Cheddar Caves. A scientist had asked for volunteers to discover if it could be the ancestor of anyone now living in the village. A schoolmaster volunteered and lo and behold his DNA proved that he was indeed a direct descendant of the skeleton. I imagine that they will soon be able to put a date – what an opportunity for a wonderful story here. Barbara had also walked down to the docks and had boarded the replica *Matthew* and was amazed to peer down and see the narrow uncomfortable planks where the 19 seamen would have to sleep – a voyage we watched breathlessly on TV. What wonderful courage and fortitude our ancestors possessed and what sense of adventure must have compelled them to face those huge unknown oceans. I do not belittle the adventuring free spirit of those contemporary heroes who went to the Moon and back, but they were sustained by everything modern science could provide, the men of the past had only their own spirit and faith to sustain them.

Recently I took a great interest in the arrival of the comet, that vast object which could have destroyed the universe and which was ignored by

116

the huge official telescopes only to be noted by two ordinary citizens in their back gardens and named Hale-Bopp.

There was a specially exciting visit one Sunday to the house in Gloucestershire where I was born. Jann and Iain drove down from Surrey and picked me up in a crashing thunderstorm, lightning flashed and torrential rain turned roads into rivers. Fortunately Iain was driving his Range Rover which towered high above the waterlogged roads while other cars sat forlornly stationary along the edges. After many vicissitudes the house is now owned by a delightful couple, the Hales, who love the place and are restoring it to its earlier beauty. It has really changed little since I lived there, the Hales now use our dining room as their sitting room and it is still papered with the correct Regency pink. The view is still superb, stretching without a single house in view right across to Wales. Miraculously the sun came out during lunch so Jann and Iain could enjoy the vista and mount the stairs to the loft – which I remember used to smell of apples – where the Hales' two sons now sleep. And so I seemed to be back where I started.

Alas, an acquaintance has recently received a card – from all places, Rome – with the words, "Pissed every night, fucking marvellous." Can this be the epitaph for Man's thousands of years of struggle and achievement?

No, the curtain thunders down –
BELOVÉD SHAKESPEARE IS HAILED MILLENNIUM MAN.

List of Subscribers

Daniel & Vanessa Abramson
Deborah Adams
Sally Adams
Mr & Mrs Antony Alderson
Pam & Jimmy Allcock
Stephen Allcock
Mrs Michael Allen
Olive Andow
Diana & John Armstrong
George Ashwood
Anne Bannister
Micky Barnard
Bob & Ann Bassett
Peggy Batchelor
Mr & Mrs G Beauchamp
Carole, David, Lisa & Lee
  Bennett
The Rt.Hon. The Lord Biffen
Sheila Bisset
Juliet Blomfield
Mrs Georgie Bodman
Mr & Mrs Douglas Brearley
Victoria Bremner
Paul Bower & Albert Brown
Katie & Robert Boyle
Odette Breen
Mrs Pat Browne
Mrs H L Burgess
Kay & Dennis Bushell
Margaret Carl & Peter Hibbs
David Childs
Paul Childs

Mrs Toni Cleton-Deane Jones
John R Cleverdon
Eleanor Coë
Peter & Julie Coë
Jennifer Coghlan
Shirley & Patrick Collins
Mary & Lucie Comer
S J Courage
Claire Crossley (née Wilesmith)
Diana Cutler (née Tippett)
Martin Davies
Robert Davies
Eileen Overholt Davis
Michael Dickman
Sylvia Dobbins
Nigel & Alison Dodd
Meryl Duff (née Humphreys)
Diana, Lady Eardley-Wilmot
Elizabeth Mary Eddy
Priscilla Eddy
Elizabeth & Francesca, in praise of
  a remarkable teacher
Lynn Farleigh
Mrs Mary Ferguson
Ian Ferguson
Terence & Sarah Fernandes
Evelynne Fisher
William & Violet Flint
David & Anne Foot
John & Sue Gallaugher
Nicholas Garrett
D V Gibbs

Michael Gibbs
Hedley Goodall
Hermione Grey
Mary & John Griffin
Joyce Grylls (née Hancock) &
    Honor Grylls
Cecily Hadley
John & Kath Hale
Mr & Mrs Nigel Hankey
Sylvia & Trevor Hannah
Emma Hardie
Carolyn Harman
Cecily Harrison & godson Mark
Tony & Katie Harrison
Doris Hart
Pam Hartly-Hodder, Gerry & Judy
    Smith
Mrs Joan Hawkins
Alan Heaton-Ward
Mrs G M Hebblethwaite MBE
Joy Hedges
Charles H Henden, Hon.G.S.M.
    (Examinations Director
    G.S.M.&D. 1964–1981)
Betty, Lady Hicks
David Higson
Yvonne & John Higson
Wally Hodge
Margaret Hogan
Rex & Dee Holdsworth
Olga Hooper
Notty Hornblower
Miss Jean Howell
Barbara Ivey
Gill James
Gwenith James
John James
Barbara Jefford OBE
Sylvia Jordan-Shore

Deborah Kerr CBE
Jacqueline M Kimber, B.Ed,
    L.G.S.M., L.L.A.M.(Hons)
Jennie Klein
Kurt & Diana Klein
Robert Klein
Thomas Klein
Prebendary & Mrs Knapman
Josephine Lawlor
Mr & Mrs T V Lawson
Nicholas Le Prevost
Audrey Leyland
Henrietta & Gary Lightwood
Sarah Lucas
Mrs J MacDonald
Anne Malone
Ann Manners (née Collins)
David & Sally March
John E Marks
L M Mears
David Mills
Terry & Mollie Milton
Michael Mollan
June Monkhouse
Suzi Nash
Mrs M Neale
Maureen Nicholls
George & Audrey Nichols
Pam
Joanne Pearce
Richard & Jane Pedlar
Mrs Helen Peplow
Sue Patrick (née White)
Anthea Peck (née Morris)
Pisces and Rob
Jean Pitt
Jean Poeton
Cyrileen Power
Dr Paul Ranger

June Rayner
Felicity Rea
Beryl M Rideout
Ula Rigg
Yvonne Robins
Mrs Harriet C Robinson
Brigid Roffe-Silvester
Pam Ruddock
Merry Rushton
John & Angela Sansom
David Sharp
Barbara Smith
Mr & Mrs James Spencer (née
   Karen Wilkinson)
Janeen Stahl
John R B Steadman
Peter & Rita Steel (née Wilce)
Sarah-Jane Stephens (née Bickerton)

Jill & Roger Stevenson
Peter Stoppard
Rita Strange
Mary Summerill
Joliette Tabb BSc
Mr & Mrs Roger Taylor
Philip Thrupp
Clifford & Ingeborg Tilley
Harry Towb & Diana Hoddinott
Jacqueline Tuckfield
Drs Stuart & Linda Tyfield
Jeremy & Monica Watkins
Frank & Linda J Webber
Barbara Weeks
Diane White
Dick & Joyce Wilkins
Pat, Tex, Kim, Tracy & Kirk
   Woodward